Constitutions, Taxation, and Land Policy

Constitutions, Taxation, and Land Policy

Abstracts of Federal and State Constitutional Constraints on the Power of Taxation Relating to Land-Planning Policy

Michael M. Bernard
Lincoln Institute of Land Policy

Lexington Books
D.C. Heath and Company
Lexington, Massachusetts
Toronto

Library of Congress Cataloging in Publication Data

Bernard, Michael M.
    Constitutions, taxation, and land policy.

    1. Real property and taxation—United States. 2. Land use—Law and legislation—United States. 3. United States—Constitutional law. I. Title.
KF6535.B47   343'.73'054   78-24792
ISBN 0-669-02823-1

Copyright © 1979 by D.C. Heath and Company

All rights reserved. No part of this publication may be reproduced or transmitted in any form or by any means, electronic or mechanical, including photocopy, recording, or any information storage or retrieval system, without permission in writing from the publisher.

Published simultaneously in Canada

Printed in the United States of America

International Standard Book Number: 0-669-02823-1

Library of Congress Catalog Card Number: 78-24792

Contents

Special Foreword on California's Proposition 13 (Jarvis-Gann Initiative) Amendment *Arlo Woolery* — vii

Introduction — 1

    Scope of the Larger Research Study — 1
    What This Reference Work Contains — 1
    How to Use This Reference Work — 2
    Tax Policy and Current Land Planning Issues — 3

Federal Constitution Abstracts — 5

State (and Commonwealth) Constitution Abstracts — 9

1.	Alabama	11
2.	Alaska	17
3.	Arizona	18
4.	Arkansas	20
5.	California	24
6.	Colorado	31
7.	Connecticut	34
8.	Delaware	35
9.	Florida	37
10.	Georgia	39
11.	Hawaii	46
12.	Idaho	47
13.	Illinois	49
14.	Indiana	52
15.	Iowa	53
16.	Kansas	54
17.	Kentucky	56
18.	Louisiana	59
19.	Maine	63
20.	Maryland	64
21.	Massachusetts	65
22.	Michigan	67
23.	Minnesota	69
24.	Mississippi	70
25.	Missouri	72
26.	Montana	76
27.	Nebraska	77

28.	Nevada	79
29.	New Hampshire	81
30.	New Jersey	82
31.	New Mexico	85
32.	New York	87
33.	North Carolina	89
34.	North Dakota	91
35.	Ohio	93
36.	Oklahoma	95
37.	Oregon	98
38.	Pennsylvania	100
39.	(Puerto Rico)	102
40.	Rhode Island	103
41.	South Carolina	104
42.	South Dakota	107
43.	Tennessee	109
44.	Texas	111
45.	Utah	115
46.	Vermont	118
47.	Virginia	119
48.	Washington	123
49.	West Virginia	126
50.	Wisconsin	128
51.	Wyoming	129

Tables of Additional Citations — 131

Due Process and Equal Protection Clauses — 133
Prohibitions against Special Privileges or Immunities — 135
Prohibitions against Excessive Fines — 136
Separation of Powers Requirements — 137
Municipal Charters and Home Rule Provisions — 138

Appendix A Summary of Proposition 13 (Jarvis-Gann Initiative) Amendment to Art. XIII A of the California Constitution *Arlo Woolery* — 139

Appendix B New Constitutional Amendments (to Beginning of 1979) — 141

About the Author — 162

Special Foreword on California's Proposition 13 (Jarvis-Gann Initiative) Amendment

On June 6, 1978, the voters of the state of California by a nearly two-to-one majority approved a sweeping change in the taxation provisions of the constitution of the state of California. This was one of the most dramatic popular actions in recent American history, and its immediate effect would be a substantial reduction in the property tax burden on the people of California. It is estimated that property taxes will be cut from $12 billion to $5 billion a year under the provisions of "Proposition 13."

If the world were a simple place and living in it were a simple process, the California taxpayers could just take the $7 billion saving and use it for whatever personal gratifications $7 billion will buy each year. However, the world is not a simple place and living in it is not a simple process, and $7 billion of lost revenue in state and local government is certain to cause some dislocations.

The full results of Proposition 13 will not be apparent immediately. We may be a long time in finding out whether all the benefits promised by the proponents of Proposition 13 actually develop. The promises of lower rents, lower taxes, and lower utility bills coupled with great increases in disposable income make persuasive preelection arguments. However, everything has its price. Miracle cures for fiscal ills also have side effects. What follows is an attempt to analyze Proposition 13 in terms of what it says, what it does, and what price it may exact from California residents in terms of its many potential side effects.

Intergovernmental Effects

Proposition 13 is anti-local government because it removes a large amount of revenue-generating capacity from local governments. The alternatives will be increased dependence on state and federal government funding or reduced local spending. If state governments provide local governments with funds for programs, those same governments are likely to exercise a large measure of control over the structure and execution of those programs.

Many federal government programs of financial assistance to local governments are based on the tax effort or providing of matching funds by those local governments. To the extent that Proposition 13 manifests itself as reduced tax effort in the property tax area and provides less revenue for matching funds, federal government funds may be curtailed for many necessary and desirable local government projects.

Impact on the Poor and Minority Groups

If, as many of its opponents suggest, Proposition 13 results in a general curtailment of public services, the first to suffer will be members of low-income and racial minority groups. These people may not be able to substitute private services for the public services that they are currently receiving from tax-supported programs. If local governments institute user charges or fees for programs that are currently funded from general tax revenues, the poor and minorities are less likely to be able to afford these fees and to be able to maintain the level of services they now enjoy through programs funded from general tax revenues. Many local governments have instituted special programs of education for minority groups. If there is an overall cutback in educational funding, many of these special programs that benefit minority groups stand a good chance of being the first to be deleted.

Political Aspects

There are several provisions in Proposition 13 that are anti-majority rule and that run counter to principles of a democratic society. One of these requires a two-thirds vote of all members elected to each of the two houses of the legislature to increase tax revenues by increasing rates or changing methods of computation. This means that a no vote by one-third of the members elected to either house of the legislature can defeat any legislation that would increase tax revenues by increasing rates or changing methods of computation. At the local level governments can impose new taxes only if approved by a two-thirds vote of the qualified electors. This means that if one-third of the qualified electors choose to stay away from the polls in any election on new taxation, the proposal would automatically be defeated. The low voter turnout in recent elections points up the difficulty of getting any change in taxation through local elections.

Benefits for Nonresident Property Owners

Proposition 13 should be a boon to non-California residents who own property in California, since they will be direct recipients of whatever tax cuts are brought about by its adoption. There is also little likelihood of their being forced to pay any type of alternative tax or suffering any direct discomfort from curtailment of public services in California communities in which they own property. If these people are living in high-property-tax states, there will be a natural tendency to liquidate investments in those states and reinvest in California real estate. The extent to which property tax benefits under Proposition 13 are capitalized into higher property values will provide only a minor deterrent to this type of tax-induced change in real estate investment decisions.

Fiscal Impacts on Different Levels of Government

Proposition 13 is mixed in its impact on state government. It invites state government to assume control of what have previously been local government programs. Programs that are regarded as absolute necessities and that can no longer be funded from the reduced local property tax revenues will have to be funded from state general funds. Along with the increased demand for state funding will inevitably come state control of those local programs and consequent growth in state government.

Proposition 13 is certainly pro-federal government in that those who pay property taxes in California will be paying substantially greater income taxes to the federal government since they will be claiming smaller deductions for property tax payments. While no one knows exactly what the increased income tax payments to the federal government will be, analysts have estimated it may exceed a billion dollars annually.

Fiscal Impacts on California Residents

Californians face another financial hazard. Many of the alternatives to property tax revenues will represent charges that are not tax deductible, so people may have to pay nondeductible user fees to obtain local services that are currently provided out of deductible, local property tax payments. However, these fees or charges will not be allowable deductions on either the state or federal income tax returns, and as a result there will be increased net costs for a fairly large number of users of those services that had hitherto been paid for out of property tax revenues.

Property owners may find themselves paying higher insurance charges if indeed the threats of municipalities to curtail police and fire protection are carried out. This is another nondeductible charge for the homeowner for tax purposes. Obviously, increased insurance costs for rental property will be expensed and deducted as a federal and state income tax deduction. However, the homeowner will not have this benefit, and the carrying cost of his housing will be increased by the amount of any increase in insurance premiums in response to diminished police and fire protection.

Land Policy Impacts

In the area of pure land policy, if we examine just the basic problem of providing housing, it is quite possible that Proposition 13, contrary to expectations, may result in reduced housing construction. If property tax capitalization works the way economists say it does, property tax savings should be capitalized into higher land prices and into temporary gains for owners of improvements on the land. When this price increment is added to the normal inflationary increases and coupled with higher interest rates, a large number of potential home buyers may be priced out of the market simply because they cannot come up with the down payment required or meet the monthly carrying costs, which reflect the higher interest and principal charges.

Rental housing should follow the same general price movements as owner-occupied houses. This would indicate higher rents which would further compound the problem of providing shelter for the growing population of the nation's most populous state.

Many other pure land policy impacts are immediately apparent in the wake of Proposition 13. Since bonding capacity is limited to a fixed percentage of assessed value, local governments' capacity for bonding to acquire land and construct improvements could be severely limited under the property tax base and rate restrictions of Proposition 13. The growth of the property tax base would be restricted to 2 percent per year plus new construction and increments due to revaluations brought about by changes of ownership under the provisions of Proposition 13. Under these restraints the property tax base, which determines bonding capacity, would be severely restricted, and local government spending for land acquisition and construction of improvements would also be severely limited.

Again, in the area of pure land policy, Proposition 13 could serve as a real incentive to buy land and hold it out of development for long periods of time. It is estimated that more than 40 percent of the taxable real estate in California is in land value. With property taxes limited to 1 percent of the indexed value from the 1975 base year, few holders of vacant or underimproved land will be under any real tax pressure to develop vacant land or upgrade existing improvements in order to create income to pay property taxes. This means a longer time horizon for land investors and less available land for current development purposes at reasonable prices.

Property Tax Equity Issues

At a time when there is dialogue at all levels of government about fair taxation, the assessors in California will be forced to administer a property tax program that has serious inequities mandated by the provisions of Proposition 13. The first of these inequities arises when like properties in the same geographical area are sold or when there is an ownership change of some kind. These sold properties will be revalued for property tax purposes at the current selling price, which could be substantially greater than the 1975 value indexed upward 2 percent annually that appears on the assessor's records. Identical properties, side by side, could have substantially different tax burdens if one of them was sold recently and the other had been in the same ownership since 1975. Also, over time, different types of properties will change in value at different rates. These differential value changes will be completely obscured by the 2 percent annual increment allowed under Proposition 13.

There is also the very real and unsought possibility that homeowners in the aggregate will be paying a disproportionately large share of the reduced total of property taxes to be collected under the provisions of Proposition 13. Residential property generally has a great deal more turnover in the marketplace than commercial and industrial property. This means that over a ten- or fifteen-year period, even with the tax incentive to avoid transfer, a substantial percentage of the homes in California will very likely be sold and placed on the tax rolls at their selling price as of the date of sale. The provisions of Proposition 13 virtually ensure that a substantially smaller percentage of commercial and industrial properties will be sold in that same period. Thus, year by year as the number of residential sales outrun the number of commercial and industrial sales, homeowners will be paying a larger and larger portion of the property tax in California.

Development Impacts

It is still too early to judge the impact of Proposition 13 on the development of public transportation. However, if new public transportation systems were to be financed by local bond issues, obviously the curtailment of the property tax base will affect bonding capacity and hence the development of public transportation. This curtailment will in turn affect the development patterns of cities and towns. The severity of this curtailment will depend to a certain extent on the overall energy situation. If we do have another severe shortage of gasoline with increased demands for mass transit, the value of property well serviced by public transportation will change relative to that of property that has limited access to convenient public transportation facilities. While these transportation-based value changes will be immediately apparent in the marketplace, they will not be reflected in the property tax base unless there happens to be a change of ownership of the affected properties.

One of the controlling factors in the development of cities and towns is the availability of sewer and water service. In areas where there have been moratoria on sewer connections, building has come to a complete standstill, and existing housing stock has greatly increased in price due to the resulting monopoly situation. To the extent that Proposition 13 has diminished the general obligation bonding capacity of local governments, there will be curtailments of municipally provided sewer and water service. This could be a real constraint on new housing construction in affected areas. This constraint could in turn inhibit the flow of outside capital into California for housing development. In fact, it might result in a reversal; available capital within California would have to go out of state to find investment opportunities in the housing field.

Prospects for Rent Control

Something must be said about the specter of rent control and its counterproductive effects as far as assessed values and housing availability are concerned. To the extent that Proposition 13 is perceived as a windfall for landlords, since property taxes on their rental properties would be lower, a call for passing the property tax saving to tenants in the form of reduced rents is inevitable. This type of thinking assumes a monopoly situation in rental housing. In a competitive housing market any pass-through would be automatic under the rental pricing system imposed by market forces. If, however, California has planned and zoned and environmentally controlled itself into a monopoly in rental housing, there may indeed be a widespread outcry for rent control. Rent control has its own pernicious effect on housing availability and on people's overall mobility. Where rent control is in effect, people become locked into geographic locations simply because of low rent. They may refuse to take advantage of employment and other opportunities in different geographical areas simply because they do not feel safe in foregoing the controlled low rents in their existing homes and risking the possibility of higher rents in areas providing greater opportunities.

If rent control is one of the fallouts of the enactment of Proposition 13, it is predictable that the California rental housing stock will follow that of England and France and other countries where widespread experiments in rent control have been attempted. In England and France most analysts agree that rent control has been a disaster, and, if anything, it has had a completely counterproductive effect. The rental housing stock has been reduced in both quantity and quality. Rent control also has the effect of encouraging overconsumption of housing in families whose children are grown and gone and encourages overcrowding in circumstances where young couples are just beginning a family. While the sponsors of Proposition 13 would be unlikely to advocate any move toward public rental housing, that has been the outcome of rent control in areas where it has been in effect for a long time.

Conclusion

People seldom react in precisely predictable ways to economic, political, or even physical stimuli. Different provisions of Proposition 13 suggest contradictory responses. The extent to which these contradictory responses offset each other will determine the net effect of Proposition 13 on investment decisions, housing availability, and overall impact on residents and taxpayers in the state of California.

Since the California voters approved Proposition 13 by a two-to-one majority, they must have found the promises of the proponents more credible than the dire warnings of the opponents. The fact that the provisions of Proposition 13 have many negative aspects and give rise to many bad results does not mean that the voters were wrong. Rather the unpredicted voter response should be interpreted as a growing disenchantment with elected representatives and a venting of pent-up frustrations over their politician's propensity for increased taxing and spending as a routine matter.

It should be pointed out in fairness, that many of the things discussed are independent problems with their own shortcomings, and they are not necessarily problems of Proposition 13 itself. However, Proposition 13 is in the process of triggering a series of responses that must generally be regarded as bad when measured against what is commonly accepted as good land policy.

Cambridge, Massachusetts
1978

Arlo Woolery
Executive Director,
Lincoln Institute of
Land Policy

Introduction

Scope of the Larger Research Study

We are all familiar enough with the revenue-raising functions of taxation, yet there is another very important aspect that has always accompanied the basic effort to raise money for the operation of government: the potentially powerful *regulatory* effect of taxing measures. Perhaps in no instance is this more dramatic than where land and other interests in real property are concerned. It seemed interesting that this matter had been raised time and again at discussions about the implementation of land policy and more often than not dismissed with a vague reference to constitutional (or legal) "constraints" on the use of the power of taxation as an instrument of land planning policy.

During one of the early seminars of the Lincoln Institute of Land Policy in Cambridge, Massachusetts, the matter again came under discussion, and it seemed most appropriate at that time to do something concrete about the need to develop a better understanding of what those legal constraints really were. In other words, not just ad hoc determinations for given jurisdictions, but a reasonably complete summary of the kinds of limitations that were to be found in the various government jurisdictions throughout the country. This need has resulted in the initiation of a larger study of legal constraints of which this publication is the first part and the first published product.

To arrive at a fuller understanding of the legal framework under which the power of taxation operates as a regulatory device, it is necessary to understand the nature of both the federal and state taxing power and its sources. Thus the pertinent provisions of federal and state constitutions must be identified. This has in fact been the first step. Next, the related constitutional case law for each area needs to be identified, together with the all-important decisions dealing with the intergovernmental relationships and distributions of the taxing and police powers. The final and more extensive portion must deal with the statutory provisions at both the federal and state levels of government and the various delegations of the authority to tax (and regulate) as they apply to land and real property interests generally. Here, too, the related case law must be examined.

What This Reference Work Contains

This initial work contains abstracts of the pertinent provisions dealing with the power of taxation, principally as that power affects real property, to be found in the U.S. Constitution and the fifty existing state constitutions. A fifty-second constitution included in this volume is that of Puerto Rico, which exists in a commonwealth status as a result of a compact relationship with the United States. Since Puerto Rico has initiated some very significant tax programs, it offers many interesting legal comparisons for our governmental system.

The constitutional abstracts following those of the federal constitution have been arranged in alphabetical order with the most current citation to the principal provisions. These have been carefully edited to their essentials in the interest of manageability and brevity and to focus on the specific subject matter relating to real property. In view of this special focus and again in the interest of brevity, provisions dealing with bonding and financing have for the most part been excluded.

Where clause headings or titles exist they have usually been included unless, for example, subject matter has been edited out. In each instance the date of enactment of the basic constitution is shown in parentheses after the name of the jurisdiction. Where substantial reforms have been made to the constitution, or a significant renumbering of the clauses has taken place, the date of this revision has also been shown.

In some instances certain constitutional provisions are so similar that they are best shown simply by citation in tabular form. These tables are found at the end of the reference work. Also, a table of citations has been included referring to municipal charter and home rule provisions, since these deal generally with local governmental interrelationships and their text does not here bear inclusion.

Anyone familiar with the classic study, *Constitutional Uniformity and Equality in State Taxation* (University of Michigan Legal Studies, 1959) by Prof. Wade Newhouse, will recognize these abstracts as something of a greatly expanded and updated version of his Appendix entitled, *Compilation of Constitutional Provisions.* Seen in this same perspective, this work is in fact intended to ultimately serve as the appendix to the larger research study that has already been described.

How to Use This Reference Work

Those who employ this reference work will find it especially valuable in making quick comparisons between the constitutional provisions of the various jurisdictions on a particular subject. In this regard, it is well to be aware of the fact that some constitutions contain nothing at all on a subject, thus leaving the matter in question open to interpretations of "absolute" sovereignty by the courts. On the other hand—and to the other extreme—some constitutions will be found to have several provisions dealing with the same subject, and at that, not always consistently. Constitutional provisions are in truth often developed by accretion as opposed to comprehensive revision, leaving the job of sorting out and integration for the courts to pursue. The prime example of this tendency will be found where uniformity and equality clauses are concerned, a matter that has

Introduction

been the subject of extensive comment, even resulting in their being collectively referred to as uniformity and equality "structures."

Although the material has been heavily edited in a number of instances as indicated, most of the essential language dealing with constitutional constraints on the power of taxation relating to real property has been included. Parenthetically, the question of what is to be considered a constitutional "constraint" to the power of taxation might best be viewed in the following way: If the power of taxation is inherent in sovereignty, then all constitutional provisions that treat with it are technically, or potentially, "constraints" on it. Thus the absence of a provision may be just as significant as its presence, if not more so.

Anyone who has attempted to find an up-to-date copy of any constitution will quickly appreciate the value of having particular, updated subject matter from all the constitutions in the country, where they can be readily compared. The separation of this portion of the study from the main work is thus intended to afford a wider utility and convenience in the use of the research product. If the unedited text of any of the provisions is needed, the correct current constitutional citation can conveniently lead one to it in the official sources. Also, updating can be achieved for subsequent changes in all the constitutions, uniformly from the June 1978 cutoff date.

It should be kept in mind that in addition to reference to the abstracted text of the state constitutions, reference should also be made to the tables described, at the end of the work, for any citations to clauses that tend to be similar in language, such as "equal protection" or "due process," that may not have been abstracted.

Court decisions relating to any of the abstracted provisions may be traced by reference to the particular state's annotated reporter system, which will contain copies of the state's constitution, with pocket-part additions. For the U.S. Constitution similar reference may be made to the federal annotated reporters; however, in the author's experience, reference to the Congressional Research Service-Library of Congress edition of *The Constitution of the United States of America* can be particularly valuable. The principal cases will be summarized and more fully discussed in a subsequent portion of the study.

Tax Policy and Current Land Planning Issues

The publication of this material at this particular time has special significance in view of the Jarvis-Gann Initiative Amendment to the constitution of the state of California, the so-called "Proposition 13", which places limits on real estate taxation on the basis of a percentage of assessed value. This measure is in fact the last constitutional enactment to be abstracted here[a] and may be seen as a

---

[a]Appendix B has been prepared at press time with the full text of new amendments in effect at the beginning of 1979.

dramatic benchmark: the beginning (or end) of an era, as it were. Although there is nothing particularly new in concept in this kind of "arithmetic" constraint, as can be observed from the abstracts, the provision has many important implications for land policy that go far beyond its initial purpose of limiting the revenue burden shouldered by the owners of real estate. As such, it is of particular interest to the policy concerns of the Lincoln Institute, and accordingly, a special foreword and appendix summary have been prepared by the Executive Director Arlo Woolery to address those problems. But the provocative inquiries of the special foreword serve only to introduce us to the importance of a number of crucial issues of tax policy as they affect land and real property generally. Others might include: What is a practical percentage ceiling to impose on property taxation that would still permit reasonable local authority and flexibility for policymaking purposes? Do many existing exemptions encourage the misuse of land? Should property be classified, and how? Should a state impose any standard of uniformity and equality beyond that required by the equal protection clause of the federal (or its own) constitution? Yet exemptions, exceptions, classification, and preferential treatment are only part of the question of the distribution of tax burdens. It will be observed that there are many other regulatory and policy-sensitive implications that need to be addressed. It is our conviction that the best place to begin the effort is through an analysis of the legal source.

Cambridge, Massachusetts *Michael M. Bernard*

Federal Constitution Abstracts

United States Constitution (1787. Rev. Bill of Rights 1791)

Art. I., § 1. All legislative Powers herein granted shall be vested in a Congress of the United States. . . .

Art. I., § 2. [cl. 3.] Representatives and direct Taxes shall be apportioned among the several States which may be included within this Union, according to their respective Numbers. . . .

Art. I., § 8. [cl. 1.] The Congress shall have Power To lay and collect Taxes, Duties, Imposts and Excises, to pay the Debts and provide for the common Defence and general Welfare of the United States; but all Duties, Imposts and Excises shall be uniform throughout the United States;

[cl. 2.] To borrow Money on the credit of the United States;

[cl. 3.] To regulate Commerce with foreign Nations, and among the several States, and with the Indian Tribes;

[cl. 5.] To coin Money, regulate the Value thereof. . . .

[cl. 17.] To exercise exclusive Legislation in all Cases whatsoever, over such District (not exceeding ten Miles square) as may, by Cession of Particular States, and the Acceptance of Congress, become the Seat of the Government of the United States, and to exercise like Authority over all Places purchased by the Consent of the Legislature of the State in which the Same shall be, for the Erection of Forts, Magazines, Arsenals, dock-Yards and other needful Buildings; —And

[cl. 18.] To make all Laws which shall be necessary and proper for carrying into Execution the foregoing Powers, and all other Powers vested by this Constitution in the Government of the United States, or in any Department or Officer thereof.

Art. I., § 9. [cl. 3.] No Bill of Attainder or ex post facto Law shall be passed.

[cl. 4.] No Capitation, or other direct, Tax shall be laid, unless in Proportion to the Census or Enumeration herein before directed to be taken.

[cl. 5.] No Tax or Duty shall be laid on Articles exported from any State.

. . . .

Art. I., § 10. [cl. 1.] No State shall . . . coin Money; emit Bills of Credit . . . pass any Bill of Attainder, ex post facto Law, or Law impairing the Obligation of Contracts. . . .

The Constitution of 1787 follows the text of the Literal Print.

[cl. 2.] No State shall, without the Consent of the Congress, lay any Imposts or Duties on Imports or Exports, except what may be absolutely necessary for executing its inspection Laws: and the net Produce of all Duties and Imposts, laid by any State on Imports or Exports, shall be for the Use of the Treasury of the United States; and all such Laws shall be subject to the Revision and Controul of the Congress.

Art. II., § 3. [The President] ... shall take Care that the Laws be faithfully executed. ...

Art. IV., § 3. [cl. 1.] New States may be admitted by the Congress into this Union; but no new State shall be formed or erected within the Jurisdiction of any other State; nor any State be formed by the Junction of two or more States, or Parts of States, without the Consent of the Legislatures of the States concerned as well as of the Congress.

[cl. 2.] The Congress shall have Power to dispose of and make all needful Rules and Regulations respecting the Territory or other Property belonging to the United States; and nothing in this Constitution shall be so construed as to Prejudice any Claims of the United States, or of any particular State.

Art. VI. [cl. 2.] This Constitution, and the Laws of the United States which shall be made in Pursuance thereof; and all Treaties made, or which shall be made, under the Authority of the United States, shall be the supreme Law of the Land; and the Judges in every State shall be bound thereby; any Thing in the Constitution or Laws of any State to the Contrary notwithstanding.

Amend. [V.] No person shall be ... deprived of life, liberty, or property, without due process of law; nor shall private property be taken for public use, without just compensation.

Amend. [VIII.] Excessive bail shall not be required, nor excessive fines imposed, nor cruel and unusual punishments inflicted.

Amend. [IX.] The enumeration in the Constitution, of certain rights, shall not be construed to deny or disparage others retained by the people.

Amend. [X.] The powers not delegated to the United States by the Constitution, nor prohibited by it to the States, are reserved to the States respectively, or to the people.

Amend. XIV., § 1. ... No State shall make or enforce any law which shall abridge the privileges or immunities of citizens of the United States; nor shall any State deprive any person of life, liberty, or property, without due process of law; nor deny to any person within its jurisdiction the equal protection of the laws.

Amend. XVI. The Congress shall have power to lay and collect taxes on incomes, from whatever source derived, without apportionment among the several States, and without regard to any census or enumeration.

**State (and Commonwealth)
Constitution Abstracts**

Alabama Constitution (1901)

Art. IV, § 91. [Exemption from taxation of state, county, municipal, cemetery and certain religious, educational and charitable property.] The legislature shall not tax the property, real or personal, of the state, counties, or other municipal corporations, or cemeteries; nor lots in incorporated cities and towns, or within one mile of any city or town to the extent of one acre, nor lots one mile or more distant from such cities or towns to the extent of five acres, with the buildings thereon, when same are used exclusively for religious worship, for schools, or for purposes purely charitable.

Art. XI, § 211. [Property taxes to be assessed in exact proportion to value of property.] All taxes levied on property in this state shall be assessed in exact proportion to the value of such property, but no tax shall be assessed upon any debt for rent or hire of real or personal property, while owned by the landlord or hirer during the current year of such rental or hire, if such real or personal property be assessed at its full value.

Art. XI, § 212. [Power to levy taxes not to be delegated.] The power to levy taxes shall not be delegated to individuals or private corporations or associations.

Art. XI, § 214. [Limitation on state property tax rate.] The legislature shall not have the power to levy in any one year a greater rate of taxation than sixty-five one-hundredths of one per centum on the value of the taxable property within this state.

Art. XI, § 216. [Limitation on property tax rates of municipal corporations.] No city, town, village, or other municipal corporation, other than as provided in this article, shall levy or collect a higher rate of taxation in any one year on the property situated therein than one-half of one per centum of the value of such property as assessed for state taxation during the preceding year. . . .

Art. XI, § 217. [Property of private corporations, associations and individuals to be taxed at same rate; exception as to religious, educational and charitable property.] The property of private corporations, associations, and individuals of this state shall forever be taxed at the same rate; provided, this section shall not apply to institutions devoted exclusively to religious, educational, or charitable purposes.

Art. XII, § 221. [Payment of state license tax, etc., not to excuse payment of other privilege and license taxes.] The legislature shall not enact any law which will permit any person, firm, corporation, or association to pay a privilege, license, or other tax to the State of Alabama, and relieve him or it from the payment of all other privilege and license taxes in the state.

Art. XII, § 223. [Limitation on assessments for public improvements by municipal corporations.] No city, town, or other municipality shall make any assessment for the cost of sidewalks or street paving, or for the cost of the construction of any sewers against property abutting on such street or sidewalk so paved, or drained by such sewers, in excess of the increased value of such property by reason of the special benefits derived from such improvements.

Amend. No. 111, § 260. . . . nothing herein contained shall be so construed as to authorize the legislature to levy in any one year a greater rate of state taxation for all purposes, including schools, than sixty-five cents on each one hundred dollars' worth of taxable property. . . .

Amend. No. 111, § 269. [Special county educational taxes.] The several counties in this state shall have power to levy and collect a special tax not exceeding ten cents on each one hundred dollars of taxable property in such counties, for the support and furtherance of education in such manner as may be authorized by the legislature; provided, that the rate of such tax, the time it is to continue, and the purpose thereof, shall have been first submitted to a vote of the qualified electors of the county, and voted for by three-fifths of those voting at such election; but the rate of such special tax shall not increase the rate of taxation, state and county combined, in any one year, to more than one dollar and twenty-five cents on each one hundred dollars of taxable property; excluding, however, all special county taxes for public buildings, roads, bridges, and the payment of debts existing at the ratification of the Constitution of eighteen hundred and seventy-five.

Amend. No. 3, Art. XIX, § 1. The several counties in the state shall have power to levy and collect a special county tax not exceeding thirty cents on each one hundred dollars worth of taxable property in such counties in addition to that now authorized or that may hereafter be authorized for public school purposes . . . [voting majority of electors required].

Amend. No. 3, Art. XIX, § 2. The several school districts of any county in the state shall have power to levy and collect a special district tax not exceeding thirty cents on each one hundred dollars worth of taxable property in such district for public school purposes . . . [voting majority of electors required].

Amend. No. 23. Art. XXI, § 219 of the present Constitution is hereby annulled and set aside and hereafter the legislature of Alabama may provide for the assessment, levy and collection of a tax upon inheritances and for the levying of estate taxes not to exceed in the aggregate the amounts which may by any law of the United States be allowed to be credited against or deducted from any similar tax upon inheritances or taxes on estates assessed or levied by the United States on the same subject. . . .

Amend. No. 25. [Income Taxes.] Art. XXII. The legislature shall have the power to levy and collect taxes for state purposes on net incomes from whatever source derived within this state . . . and to designate and define the incomes to be taxed and to fix the rates of taxes, provided that the rate shall not exceed 5 percent nor 3 percent on corporations. Income shall not be deemed property for purposes of ad valorem taxes . . . The legislature shall reduce the ad valorem tax from time to time when and to such an amount as the revenue derived from the income tax will justify. . . .

Amend. No. 27, § 229. . . . The legislature shall, by general laws, provide for the payment to the state of Alabama of a franchise tax by corporations organized under the laws of this state which shall be in proportion to the amount of capital stock; but strictly benevolent, educational or religious corporations or federal building and loan associations organized pursuant to an act of congress known as the Home Owners' Loan Act of 1933, as amended, and as the same may hereafter be amended, or building and loan associations organized under or authorized to do business by the laws of Alabama shall not be required to pay such a tax on their withdrawable or repurchasable shares. . . .

Amend. No. 56. [Additional Municipal Taxes.] Each municipal corporation in this state whose annual ad valorem tax rate is otherwise limited by the Constitution or any amendment thereto less than one and one-fourth per centum (1¼ %) of the value of the property situated therein as assessed for state taxation during the preceding year shall have, in addition to the power to levy and collect such ad valorem tax each year at the rate authorized immediately prior to the adoption of this amendment, the further power to levy and collect each year an additional tax or taxes to such extent that the total ad valorem tax rate of such municipal corporation shall not exceed one and one-fourth per centum (1¼%) in any one year on the property situated therein based on the valuation of such property as assessed for state taxation during the preceding year; provided, that before any such additional tax may be so levied and collected a majority of the qualified voters of any such municipal corporation voting at an election called for that purpose shall vote in favor of the levy thereof; provided further, that the total ad valorem tax or taxes to be levied and collected by any such municipal corporation shall not exceed one and one-fourth per centum (1¼ %) in any one year; and provided further, that the adoption of this amendment shall in no wise affect, limit, modify, abridge or impair the power, authority or right of any such municipal corporation to levy and collect the special school taxes now or hereafter vested or conferred upon them, or any of them, under the Constitution or any amendment thereto, which said special school taxes shall be in excess of said one and one-fourth per centum (1¼ %) herein provided for. . . .

Amend. No. 61. §B. . . . All homesteads in Alabama are hereby declared to be exempt from all state ad valorem tax to the extent of at least $2,000.00 in assessed value....

Amend. No. 202. The court of county commissioners, board of revenue, or other like governing body of each of the several counties in the state shall have the power to levy and collect a special county tax of not to exceed fifty cents on each one hundred dollars of taxable property, in addition to all other taxes now or hereafter authorized by the Constitution and laws of Alabama, for educational purposes, on the value of the taxable property in the county as assessed for state taxation . . . [voting majority of electors required].

Amend. No. 208, § 215. No county in this state shall be authorized to levy a greater rate of taxation in any one year on the value of the taxable property therein than one-half of one per centum....

Amend. No. 212. [STATE TAX ON NET INCOME OF CORPORATIONS.] The legislature shall have power to levy and provide for the collection of taxes for state purposes on net income of corporations, from whatever source derived . . . at a rate not exceeding five percent. However, all federal income taxes paid or accrued within the taxable year by corporations shall always be deductible in computing net income taxable under the income tax laws of this state, provided that in the case of foreign corporations the amount of federal income tax deductible shall be in proportion to income derived from sources within Alabama, to be determined in accordance with such laws as the legislature may enact.

Amend. No. 325, Art. XI, § 217. [Classification of taxable property for purposes of ad valorem taxation; taxable property to be taxed by state, counties, municipalities, etc., at same rate; assessment ratios for purposes of ad valorem taxation; increase or decrease of ad valorem tax rate by counties, municipalities, etc.; exemption of state, county and municipal property and property used for religious, educational or charitable purposes from taxation; legislature may provide exemptions from taxation; interpretation of authority for counties, municipalities, etc., to levy taxes, incur indebtedness, etc., in relation to assessment of property; maximum rate of ad valorem tax in any one taxable year.]

(a) All taxable property within this state, not exempt by law, shall be divided into the following classes for the purposes of ad valorem taxation:
    Class I. All property of utilities used in the business of such utilities,
    Class II. All property not otherwise classified,
    Class III. All agricultural, forest and residential property.

(b) With respect to ad valorem taxes levied by the state, all taxable property shall be forever taxed at the same rate, and such property shall be assessed for ad valorem tax purposes according to the classes thereof as herein defined at the following ratios of assessed value to the fair and reasonable market value of such property:

Class I. 30 per centum
Class II. 25 per centum
Class III. 15 per centum

(c) With respect to ad valorem taxes levied by counties, municipalities or other taxing authority, all taxable property shall be forever taxed at the same rate, and such property shall be assessed for ad valorem tax purposes according to the classes of property defined in paragraph (a) herein and at the same ratios of assessed value to the fair and reasonable market value thereof as fixed in paragraph (b) herein, provided, however, that the legislature may vary the ratio of assessed value to the fair and reasonable market value as to any class of property as defined in paragraph (b) herein, and provided, further, that the legislature may fix a uniform ratio of assessment of all property within a county defined in paragraph (a) herein as Class II and III and may fix a different ratio of assessment for property defined in paragraph (a) as Class I. Such ratios as herein authorized may vary among counties so long as each such ratio is uniform within a county.

No class of property shall have a ratio of assessed value to fair and reasonable market value of less than 15 per centum nor more than 35 per centum.

(d) A county, municipality, or other taxing authority may decrease any ad valorem tax rate at any time, provided such decrease shall not jeopardize the payment of any bonded indebtedness secured by such tax. . . .

(e) Any county, municipality, or other taxing authority may increase the rate at which ad valorem taxes are levied above the limit now provided in the Constitution provided that the proposed increase shall have been (1) proposed by the authority having power to levy the tax after a public hearing on such proposal, (2) thereafter approved by an act of the legislature, and (3) subsequently approved by a majority vote of the qualified electors of the area in which the tax is to be levied or increased who vote on the proposal.

(f) The legislature is authorized to enact legislation to implement the provisions of this amendment, and may provide for exemptions from taxation; provided, however, that any statutory exemption existing prior to the adoption of this amendment shall not be repealed, except by subsequent legislative act, and shall remain in full force and effect.

(g) Wherever any constitutional provision or statute provides for, limits or measures the power or authority of any county, municipality or other taxing authority to levy taxes, borrow money, or incur indebtedness in relation to the assessment of property therein for state taxes or for state and county taxes such provision shall mean as assessed for county or municipal taxes as the case may be.

(h) Any provision of the Constitution of Alabama to the contrary notwithstanding, ad valorem taxes shall never exceed 1½% of the fair and reasonable market value of the property in any one taxable year.

Note: See appendix B for subsequent amendment affecting foregoing provisions enacted November 1978.

Alaska Constitution (1959)

Art. IX. FINANCE AND TAXATION

§ 1. **Taxing power.** The power of taxation shall never be surrendered. This power shall not be suspended or contracted away, except as provided in this article.

§ 2. **Non-discrimination.** The lands and other property belonging to citizens of the United States residing without the State shall never be taxed at a higher rate than the lands and other property belonging to the residents of the State.

§ 3. **Assessment standards.** Standards for appraisal of all property assessed by the State or its political subdivisions shall be prescribed by law.

§ 4. **Exemptions.** The real and personal property of the State or its political subdivisions shall be exempt from taxation under conditions and exceptions which may be provided by law. All, or any portion of, property used exclusively for non-profit religious, charitable, cemetery, or educational purposes, as defined by law, shall be exempt from taxation. Other exemptions of like or different kind may be granted by general law. All valid existing exemptions shall be retained until otherwise provided by law.

§ 5. **Interests in government property.** Private leaseholds, contracts, or interests in land or property owned or held by the United States, the State, or its political subdivisions, shall be taxable to the extent of the interests.

§ 6. **Public purpose.** No tax shall be levied, or appropriation of public money made, or public property transferred, nor shall the public credit be used, except for a public purpose.

§ 7. **Dedicated funds.** The proceeds of any state tax or license shall not be dedicated to any special purpose, except as provided in Sec. 15[a] of this Article or when required by the federal government for state participation in federal programs. This provision shall not prohibit the continuance of any dedication for special purposes existing upon the date of ratification of this constitution by the people of Alaska.

Art. X. LOCAL GOVERNMENT

§ 2. **Local government powers.** All local government powers shall be vested in boroughs and cities. The State may delegate taxing powers to organized boroughs and cities only.

---

[a] Sec. 15 provides for an Alaska Permanent Fund for Mineral Royalties, etc.

Arizona Constitution (1912)

Art. IV, Pt. 2, § 19. Local or special laws. No local or special laws shall be enacted in any of the following cases, that is to say:

. . . .

9. Assessment and collection of taxes.

. . . .

Art. IX, § 1. Surrender of power of taxation; uniformity of taxes. The power of taxation shall never be surrendered, suspended, or contracted away. All taxes shall be uniform upon the same class of property within the territorial limits of the authority levying the tax, and shall be levied and collected for public purposes only.

Art. IX, § 2. Tax exemptions. There shall be exempt from taxation all federal, state, county and municipal property. Property of educational, charitable and religious associations or institutions not used or held for profit may be exempt from taxation by law. . . . There shall be further exempt from taxation the property of widows, honorably discharged soldiers, sailors, United States marines . . . residents of this state, not exceeding the amount of two thousand dollars, where the total assessment of such widow and such other persons named herein does not exceed five thousand dollars. . . . All property in the state not exempt under the laws of the United States or under this constitution, or exempt by law under the provisions of this section shall be subject to taxation, to be ascertained as provided by law. This section shall be self-executing.

Art. IX, § 3. The Legislature shall provide by law for an annual tax sufficient, with other sources of revenue, to defray the necessary ordinary expenses of the State for each fiscal year. . . .

No tax shall be levied except in pursuance of law, and every law imposing a tax shall state distinctly the object of the tax, to which object only it shall be applied. . . .

Art. IX, § 6. Local assessments and taxes. Incorporated cities, towns, and villages may be vested by law with power to make local improvements by special assessments, or by special taxation of property benefited. For all corporate purposes, all municipal corporations may be vested with authority to assess and collect taxes.

Art. IX, § 9. Statement of tax and objects. Every law which imposes, continues, or revives a tax shall distinctly state the tax and the objects for which it shall be applied; and it shall not be sufficient to refer to any other law to fix such tax or object.

Art. IX, § 10. Aid of church, private or sectarian school, or public service corporation. No tax shall be laid or appropriation of public money made in aid of any church, or private or sectarian school, or any public service corporation.

Art. IX, § 11. From and after December 31, 1973, the manner, method and mode of assessing, equalizing and levying taxes in the State of Arizona shall be such as is prescribed by law. . . .

. . . [M]obile homes, as defined by law for tax purposes, shall not be subject to the license tax imposed under the provisions of this section but shall be subject to ad valorem property taxes on any mobile homes in the manner provided by law. . . .

Art. IX, § 12. Authority to provide for levy and collection of license and other taxes. The law-making power shall have authority to provide for the levy and collection of license, franchise, gross revenue, excise, income, collateral and direct inheritance, legacy, and succession taxes, also graduated income taxes, graduated collateral and direct inheritance taxes, graduated legacy and succession taxes, stamp, registration, production, or other specific taxes.

Art. XX. ORDINANCE
The following ordinance shall be irrevocable without the consent of the United States and the people of this State:
. . . Fifth. **Taxation.** The lands and other property belonging to citizens of the United States residing without this State shall never be taxed at a higher rate than the lands and other property situated in this State belonging to residents thereof. . . .

Arkansas Constitution (1874)

Art. II, § 23. [Eminent domain and taxation.] The State's ancient right of eminent domain and of taxation is herein fully and expressly conceded and the General Assembly may delegate the taxing power with the necessary restriction, to the State's subordinate political and municipal corporations to the extent of providing for their existence, maintenance and well being, but no further.

Art. V, § 31. [Purposes of taxes and appropriations.] No State tax shall be allowed, or appropriation of money made, except to raise means for the payment of the just debts of the State, for defraying the necessary expenses of government, to sustain common schools, to repel invasion and suppress insurrection, except by a majority of two-thirds of both houses of the General Assembly.

Art. XII, § 3. [Cities and towns; organization under general laws.] The General Assembly shall provide, by general laws, for the organization of cities (which may be classified) and incorporated towns, and restrict their power of taxation, assessment, borrowing money and contracting debts, so as to prevent the abuse of such power.

Art. XII, § 4. [Limitation on legislative and taxing power.] No municipal corporation shall be authorized to pass any laws contrary to the general laws of the State; nor levy any tax on real or personal property to a greater extent, in one year, than five mills on the dollar of the assessed value of the same. . . .

Art. XVI, § 5. [Property taxed according to value; license taxes; tax exemptions.] All property subject to taxation shall be taxed according to its value, that value to be ascertained in such manner as the General Assembly shall direct, making the same equal and uniform throughout the State. No one species of property from which a tax may be collected shall be taxed higher than another species of property of equal value provided the General Assembly shall have power from time to time to tax . . . exhibitions and privileges in such manner as may be deemed proper. Provided, further, that the following property shall be exempt from taxation: Public property used exclusively for public purposes; churches used as such; cemeteries used exclusively as such; school buildings and apparatus; libraries and grounds used exclusively for school purposes, and buildings and grounds and materials used exclusively for public charity.

Art. XVI, § 6. [Other tax exemptions forbidden.] All laws exempting property from taxation other than as provided in this Constitution shall be void.

Art. XVI, § 7. [Taxation of corporate property.] The power to tax corporations and corporate property shall not be surrendered or suspended by any contract or grant to which the State may be a party.

Art. XVI, § 8. [Maximum rate of state taxes.] The General Assembly shall not have power to levy State taxes for any one year to exceed in aggregate one per cent of the assessed valuation of the property of the State for that year.

Art. XVI, § 9. [County taxes; limitation.] No county shall levy a tax to exceed one-half of one per cent for all purposes, but may levy an additional one-half of one per cent to pay indebtedness existing at the time of the ratification of this Constitution.

Art. XVI, § 11. [Levy and appropriation of taxes.] No tax shall be levied except in pursuance of law, and every law imposing a tax shall state distinctly the object of the same; and no moneys arising from a tax levied for one purpose shall be used for any other purpose.

Art. XIX, § 27. [Local improvements; municipal assessments.] Nothing in this Constitution shall be so construed as to prohibit the General Assembly from authorizing assessments on real property for local improvements in towns and cities under such regulations as may be prescribed by law to be based upon the consent of a majority in value of the property holders owning property adjoining the locality to be affected; but such assessments shall be ad valorem and uniform.

Amend. No. 12. Cotton Mills Tax Exempt for Seven Years. All capital invested in a textile mill in this State for the manufacture of cotton and fiber goods in any manner shall be and is hereby declared to be exempt from taxation for a period of seven years from the date of the location of said textile mill.

Amend. No. 18. Tax to Aid Industries. It being most apparent that factories, industries and transportation facilities are necessary for the development of a community and for the welfare of its inhabitants, a special tax not exceeding five mills on the dollar of all taxable property in cities of the first class located in counties now or hereafter having not less than one hundred five thousand population, in addition to other taxes now provided by law, may be levied in such cities for the period that may be provided by law, when petitioned for by ten per cent of the owners of real property in such cities and on consent of a majority of the electors of such city voting on the question. . . .

The proceeds of such tax may be expended as may be provided by law for the purpose of securing the location of factories, industries, river transportation and facilities therefor within and adjacent to such cities or other public purposes, exclusive of charities and those now within the powers of said city to perform, and the expenditures may also be made for . . . any other public purpose that may be provided by law, connected with securing the location of such factories and industries and encouraging them. . . .

Amend. No. 19. That Article 5[a] of the Constitution of the State of Arkansas be amended by adding thereto the following:

. . . .

§ 38. None of the rates for property, excise, privilege or personal taxes, now levied shall be increased by the General Assembly except after the approval of the qualified electors voting thereon at an election, or in the case of emergency, by the vote of three-fourths of the members elected to each House of the General Assembly.

Amend. No. 22. An Amendment to Provide for an Exemption of Homesteads from Certain State Taxes

§ 1. The homestead of each and every resident of the State, whether or not such resident be married or unmarried, male or female, shall be wholly exempt from all State taxes authorized or referred to in Section 8 of Article XVI of the Constitution of Arkansas in all cases where such homestead does not exceed the assessed valuation of One Thousand Dollars ($1,000.00). Where the assessed valuation of such homestead exceeds One Thousand Dollars ($1,000.00), this exemption shall apply to the first One Thousand Dollars ($1,000.00) of such valuation.

§ 2. Within a maximum limit of Two Thousand Five Hundred Dollars ($2,500.00) and a minimum limit of One Thousand Dollars ($1,000.00), the legislature is hereby authorized and empowered from time to time to fix the amount of the exemption hereby provided.

. . . .

Amend. No. 27. Industry Tax Exemption. The Governor and the Agricultural and Industrial Commission (or the agency created by law to assist in the industrial development of Arkansas) may investigate and contract with the owners of any new manufacturing or processing establishment to be located in the State, or owners making addition or additions to any manufacturing or processing establishment already located in the State, for the exemption from State property taxation of any such new manufacturing or processing establishment, or any addition or additions to any such existing manufacturing or processing establishment, upon such terms and conditions as the Governor and the said Commission may deem to the best interest of the State; provided, that no exemption from taxes shall be granted under this amendment for a longer period than ten (10) calendar years succeeding the date of any such contract. Any such exemption shall "ipso facto" cease upon violation of the terms and conditions of any contract hereby made.

---

[a] Art. 5 deals with general legislative powers.

Arkansas Constitution

Amend. No. 47. State Ad Valorem Tax Prohibition
§ 1. No ad valorem tax shall be levied upon property by the State.
§ 2. All provisions in the Constitution of the State of Arkansas, or in any amendment thereto, or in the statutes of the State of Arkansas in conflict herewith are hereby repealed.

Amend. No. 57.
§ 1. The General Assembly may classify intangible personal property for assessment at lower percentages of value than other property. . . .

California Constitution (1879)

Art. XI, § 11. (a) The Legislature may not delegate to a private person or body power to make, control, appropriate, supervise or interfere with county or municipal corporation improvements, money, or property, or to levy taxes or assessments, or perform municipal functions.

Art. XI, § 14. A local government formed after the effective date of this section, the boundaries of which include all or part of two or more counties, shall not levy a property tax unless such tax has been approved by a majority vote of the qualified voters of that local government voting on the issue of the tax.

Art. XIII, § 1. [Taxable property; percentage; full value.]
Unless otherwise provided by this Constitution or the laws of the United States:

(a) All property is taxable and shall be assessed at the same percentage of fair market value. When a value standard other than fair market value is prescribed by this Constitution or by statute authorized by this Constitution, the same percentage shall be applied to determine the assessed value. The value to which the percentage is applied, whether it be the fair market value or not, shall be known for property tax purposes as the full value.

(b) All property so assessed shall be taxed in proportion to its full value.

Art. XIII, § 2. . . . The tax on any interest in . . . mortgages shall not exceed four-tenths of one percent of full value, and the tax per dollar of full value shall not be higher on personal property than on real property in the same taxing jurisdiction.

Art. XIII, § 3. The following are exempt from property taxation:

(a) Property owned by the State.

(b) Property owned by a local government, except as otherwise provided. . . .

(d) Property used for libraries and museums that are free and open to the public and property used exclusively for public schools, community colleges, state colleges and state universities.

(e) Buildings, land, equipment, and securities used exclusively for educational purposes by a nonprofit institution of higher education.

(f) Buildings, land on which they are situated, and equipment used exclusively for religious worship.

(g) Property used or held exclusively for the permanent deposit of human dead or for the care and maintenance of the property or the dead, except when used or held for profit. This property is also exempt from special assessment.

(h) Growing crops.

(i) Fruit and nut trees until 4 years after the season in which they were

California Constitution

planted in orchard form and grape vines until 3 years after the season in which they were planted in vineyard form.

(j) Immature forest trees planted on lands not previously bearing merchantable timber. . . .

The Legislature may supersede the foregoing provisions with an alternative system or systems of taxing or exempting forest trees or timber, including a taxation system not based on property valuation. Any alternative system or systems shall provide for exemption of unharvested immature trees, shall encourage the continued use of timberlands for the production of trees for timber products, and shall provide for restricting the use of timberland to the production of timber products and compatible uses with provisions for taxation of timberland based on the restrictions. Nothing in this paragraph shall be construed to exclude timberland from the provisions of Section 8 of this article.

(k) $7,000 of the full value of a dwelling, as defined by the Legislature, when occupied by an owner as his principal residence, unless the dwelling is receiving another real property exemption. . . .

(n) Any debt secured by land.

(o) Property in the amount of $1,000 of a claimant who—

(1) is serving in or has served in and has been discharged under honorable conditions from service in the [armed services] . . . .

An unmarried person who owns property valued at $5,000 or more, or a married person, who, together with the spouse, owns property valued at $10,000 or more, is ineligible for this exemption.

If the claimant is married and does not own property eligible for the full amount of the exemption, property of the spouse shall be eligible for the unused balance of the exemption.

(p) (1) [spouse included in exemption]

(q) (1) [parent included in exemption]

Art. XIII, § 4. The Legislature may exempt from property taxation in whole or in part:

(a) The home of a person or a person's spouse [for military disability].

(b) Property used exclusively for religious, hospital, or charitable purposes and owned or held in trust by corporations or other entities (1) that are organized and operating for those purposes, (2) that are nonprofit, and (3) no part of whose net earnings inures to the benefit of any private shareholder or individual; . . . .

(d) Real property not used for commercial purposes that is reasonably and necessarily required for parking vehicles of persons worshipping on land exempt by Section 3 (f).

Art. XIII, § 5. Exemptions granted or authorized by Sections 3(e), 3(f), and 4(b) apply to buildings under construction, land required for their convenient use, and equipment in them if the intended use would qualify the property for exemption.

Art. XIII, § 7. The Legislature, two-thirds of the membership of each house concurring, may authorize county boards of supervisors to exempt real property having a full value so low that, if not exempt, the total taxes and applicable subventions on the property would amount to less than the cost of assessing and collecting them.

Art. XIII, § 8. To promote the conservation, preservation and continued existence of open space lands, the Legislature may define open space land and shall provide that when this land is enforceably restricted, in a manner specified by the Legislature, to recreation, enjoyment of scenic beauty, use for conservation of natural resources, or production of food or fiber, it shall be valued for property tax purposes only on a basis that is consistent with its restrictions and uses.

To promote the preservation of property of historical significance, the Legislature may define such property and shall provide that when it is enforceably restricted, in a manner specified by the Legislature, it shall be valued for property tax purposes only on a basis that is consistent with its restrictions and uses.

Art. XIII, § 8.5. The Legislature may provide by law for the manner in which a person of low or moderate income who is 62 years of age or older may postpone ad valorem property taxes on the dwelling owned and occupied by him as his principal place of residence. The Legislature shall have plenary power to define all terms in this section. . . .

Art. XIII, § 9. The Legislature may provide for the assessment for taxation only on the basis of use of a single-family dwelling, as defined by the Legislature, and so much of the land as is required for its convenient use and occupation, when the dwelling is occupied by an owner and located on land zoned exclusively for single-family dwellings or for agricultural purposes.

Art. XIII, § 10. Real property in a parcel of 10 or more acres which, on the lien date and for 2 or more years immediately preceding, has been used exclusively for nonprofit golf course purposes shall be assessed for taxation on the basis of such use, plus any value attributable to mines, quarries, hydrocarbon substances, or other minerals in the property or the right to extract hydrocarbons or other minerals from the property.

Art. XIII, § 12. (a) Except as provided in subdivision (b), taxes on personal property, possessory interests in land, and taxable improvements located on land exempt from taxation which are not a lien upon land sufficient in value to secure their payment shall be levied at the rates for the preceding tax year upon property of the same kind where the taxes were a lien upon land sufficient in value to secure their payment.

(b) In any year in which the assessment ratio is changed, the Legislature shall adjust the rate described in subdivision (a) to maintain equality between property on the secured and unsecured rolls.

Art. XIII, § 13. Land and improvements shall be separately assessed.

Art. XIII, § 14. All property taxed by local government shall be assessed in the county, city, and district in which it is situated.

Art. XIII, § 18. The [State Board of Equalization] shall measure county assessment levels annually and shall bring those levels into conformity by adjusting entire secured local assessment rolls. In the event a property tax is levied by the state, however, the effects of unequalized local assessment levels, to the extent any remain after such adjustments, shall be corrected for purposes of distributing this tax by equalizing the assessment levels of locally and state-assessed properties and varying the rate of the state tax inversely with the counties' respective assessment levels.

Art. XIII, § 19. The [State Board of Equalization] shall annually assess (1) pipelines, flumes, canals, ditches, and aqueducts lying within 2 or more counties and (2) property, except franchises, owned or used by regulated railway, telegraph, or telephone companies, car companies operating on railways in the State, and companies transmitting or selling gas or electricity. This property shall be subject to taxation to the same extent and in the same manner as other property.

No other tax or license charge may be imposed on these companies which differs from that imposed on mercantile, manufacturing, and other business corporations. . . .

Art. XIII, § 20. The Legislature may provide maximum property tax rates and bonding limits for local governments.

Art. XIII, § 21. Within such limits as may be provided under Section 20 of this Article, the Legislature shall provide for an annual levy by county governing bodies of school district taxes sufficient to produce annual revenues for each district that the district's board determines are required for its schools and district functions.

Art. XIII, § 22. Not more than 25 percent of the total appropriations from all funds of the State shall be raised by means of taxes on real and personal property according to the value thereof.

Art. XIII, § 24. The Legislature may not impose taxes for local purposes but may authorize local governments to impose them. . . .

Art. XIII, § 26. [Income tax; exemptions]. (a) Taxes on or measured by income may be imposed on persons, corporations, or other entities as prescribed by law.

. . . .

(c) Income of a nonprofit educational institution of collegiate grade within the State of California is exempt from taxes on or measured by income if; (1) it is not unrelated business income as defined by the Legislature, and (2) it is used exclusively for educational purposes.

Art. XIII, § 27. [Taxations of corporations and banks]. The Legislature, a majority of the membership of each house concurring, may tax corporations, including State and national banks, and their franchises by any method not prohibited by this Constitution or the Constitution or laws of the United States. Unless otherwise provided by the Legislature, the tax on State and national banks shall be according to or measured by their net income and shall be in lieu of all other taxes and license fees upon banks or their shares, except taxes upon real property and vehicle registration and license fees.

Art. XIII, § 31. The power to tax may not be surrendered or suspended by grant or contract.

Art. XIII A,[a] **§ 1.** (a) The maximum amount of any ad valorem tax on real property shall not exceed One percent (1%) of the full cash value of such property. The one percent (1%) tax to be collected by the counties and apportioned according to law to the districts within the counties.

(b) The limitation provided for in subdivision (a) shall not apply to ad valorem taxes or special assessments to pay the interest and redemption charges on any indebtedness approved by the voters prior to the time this section becomes effective.

Art. XIII A, § 2. (a) The full cash value means the County Assessors valuation of real property as shown on the 1975-76 tax bill under "full cash value", or thereafter, the appraised value of real property when purchased, newly constructed, or a change in ownership has occured [sic] after the 1975 assessment. All real property not already assessed up to the 1975-76 tax levels may be reassessed to reflect that valuation.

(b) The fair market value base may reflect from year to year the inflationary rate not to exceed two percent (2%) for any given year or reduction as shown in the consumer price index or comparable data for the area under taxing jurisdiction.

Art. XIII A, § 3. From and after the effective date of this article, any changes in State taxes enacted for the purpose of increasing revenues collected pursuant thereto whether by increased rates or changes in methods of computation must be imposed by an Act passed by not less than two-thirds of all members elected to each of the two houses of the Legislature, except that no new ad valorem taxes on real property, or sales or transaction taxes on the sales of real property may be imposed.

---

[a]This article is the so-called Jarvis-Gann Constitutional Amendment, also referred to as California's Proposition 13. It is reproduced here in its entirety. It was subsequently amended in November 1978 in §§ 2 (a) and (b). See appendix B.

Art. XIII A, § 4. Cities, Counties and special districts, by a two-thirds vote of the qualified electors of such district, may impose special taxes on such district, except ad valorem taxes on real property or a transaction tax or sales tax on the sale of real property within such City, County or special district.

Art. XIII A, § 5. This article shall take effect for the tax year beginning on July 1 following the passage of this Amendment, except Section 3 which shall become effective upon the passage of this article.

Art. XIII A, § 6. If any section, part, clause, or phrase hereof is for any reason held to be invalid or unconstitutional, the remaining sections shall not be affected but will remain in full force and effect.

Art. XVI, § 16. [Property in redevelopment project] All property in a redevelopment project established under the Community Redevelopment Law Act as now existing or hereafter amended, except publicly owned property not subject to taxation by reason of such ownership, shall be taxed in proportion to its value as provided in Section 1 of this article, and such taxes (the word "taxes" as used herein shall include, but shall not be limited to, all levies on an ad valorem basis upon land or real property) shall be levied and collected as other taxes are levied and collected by the respective taxing agencies.

The Legislature may provide that any redevelopment plan may contain a provision that the taxes, if any, so levied upon such taxable property in a redevelopment project each year by or for the benefit of the State of California, any city, county, city and county, district, or other public corporation (hereinafter sometimes called "taxing agencies") after the effective date of the ordinance approving the redevelopment plan, shall be divided as follows:

(a) That portion of the taxes which would be produced by the rate upon which the tax is levied each year by or for each of said taxing agencies upon the total sum of the assessed value of the taxable property in the redevelopment project as shown upon the assessment roll used in connection with the taxation of such property by such taxing agency, last equalized prior to the effective date of such ordinance, shall be allocated to, and when collected shall be paid into, the funds of the respective taxing agencies as taxes by or for said taxing agencies on all other property are paid (for the purpose of allocating taxes levied by or for any taxing agency or agencies which did not include the territory in a redevelopment project on the effective date of such ordinance but to which such territory has been annexed or otherwise included after such effective date, the assessment roll of the county last equalized on the effective date of said ordinance shall be used in determining the assessed valuation of the taxable property in the project on said effective date); and

(b) That portion of said levied taxes each year in excess of such amount shall be allocated to and when collected shall be paid into a special fund of the redevelopment agency.... Unless and until the total assessed valuation of the taxable property in a redevelopment project exceeds the total assessed value of the taxable property in such project as shown by the last equalized assessment roll referred to in paragraph designated (a) hereof, all the taxes levied and collected upon the taxable property in such redevelopment project shall be paid into the funds of the respective taxing agencies. . . .

Colorado Constitution (1876)

Art. V, § 35. Delegation of power. The general assembly shall not delegate to any special commission, private corporation or association, any power to... levy taxes or perform any municipal function whatever.

Art. X, § 2. Tax provided for state expenses.—The general assembly shall provide by law for an annual tax sufficient, with other resources, to defray the estimated expenses of the state government for each fiscal year.

Art. X, § 3. Uniform taxation—exemptions.—All taxes shall be uniform upon each of the various classes of real and personal property located within the territorial limits of the authority levying the tax, and shall be levied, assessed, and collected under general laws, which shall prescribe such methods and regulations as shall secure just and equalized valuations for assessments of taxes upon all property, real and personal, located within the territorial limits of the authority levying the tax....

Ditches, canals and flumes owned and used by individuals or corporations for irrigating land owned by such individuals or corporations, or the individual members thereof, shall not be separately taxed so long as they shall be owned and used exclusively for such purposes.

Art. X, § 4. Public property exempt.—The property, real and personal, of the state, counties, cities, towns and other municipal corporations and public libraries, shall be exempt from taxation.

Art. X, § 5. Public used for religious worship, schools and charitable purposes exempt.—Property, real and personal, that is used solely and exclusively for religious worship, for schools or for strictly charitable purposes, also cemeteries not used or held for private or corporate profit, shall be exempt from taxation, unless otherwise provided by general law.

Art. X, § 6. ... the general assembly shall provide by law for the taxation of mobile homes....

Art. X, § 7. Municipal taxation by general assembly prohibited.—The general assembly shall not impose taxes for the purposes of any county, city, town or other municipal corporation, but may by law, vest in the corporate authorities thereof respectively, the power to assess and collect taxes for all purposes of such corporation.

Art. X, § 8. No county, city, or town to be released.—No county, city, town or other municipal corporation, the inhabitants thereof, nor the property therein, shall be released or discharged from their or its proportionate share of taxes to be levied for state purposes.

Art. X, § 9. Relinquishment of power to tax corporations forbidden.—The power to tax corporations and corporate property, real and personal, shall never be relinquished or suspended.

Art. X, § 10. Corporations subject to tax.—All corporations in this state, or doing business therein, shall be subject to taxation for state, county, school, municipal and other purposes, on the real and personal property owned or used by them within the territorial limits of the authority levying the tax.

Art. X, § 11. Maximum rate of taxation.—The rate of taxation on property, for state purposes, shall never exceed four mills on each dollar of valuation; provided, however, that in the discretion of the general assembly an additional levy of not to exceed one mill on each dollar of valuation may from time to time be authorized for the erection of additional buildings at, and for the use, benefit, maintenance, and support of the state educational institutions; provided, further, that the rate of taxation on property for all state purposes, including the additional levy herein provided for shall never exceed five mills on each dollar of valuation, unless otherwise provided in the constitution.

Art. X, § 15. Boards of equalization—duties.—. . . As may be prescribed by law, the county boards of equalization shall raise, lower, adjust, and equalize valuations for assessment of taxes upon real and personal property located within their respective counties, subject to review and revision by the state board of equalization.

. . . As may be prescribed by law, the state board of equalization shall review the valuations determined for assessment of taxes upon the various classes of real and personal property located in the several counties of the state, and shall raise, lower and adjust the same, to the end that all valuations for assessment of taxes shall be just and equalized; provided, however, that said state board of equalization shall have no power of original assessment.

. . . .

Art. X, § 17. Income tax.—The general assembly may levy income taxes, either graduated or proportional, or both graduated and proportional, for the support of the state, or any political subdivision thereof, or for public schools, and may, in the administration of an income tax law, provide for special classified or limited taxation or the exemption of tangible and intangible personal property.

Art. XX, § 6. Home rule for cities and towns.

. . . .

From and after the certifying to and filing with the secretary of state of a charter framed and approved in reasonable conformity with the provisions of this article, such city or town, and the citizens thereof, shall have the . . . power to legislate upon, provide, regulate, conduct and control:

. . . .

g. The assessment of property in such city or town for municipal taxation and the levy and collection of taxes thereon for municipal purposes and special assessments for local improvements; such assessments, levy and collection of taxes and special assessments to be made by municipal officials or by the county or state officials as may be provided by the charter;

h. The imposition, enforcement and collection of fines and penalties for the violation of any of the provisions of the charter, or of any ordinance adopted in pursuance of the charter. . . .

Connecticut Constitution (1965)

Art. I, § 1. Equality of rights. All men when they form a social compact, are equal in rights; and no man or set of men are entitled to exclusive public emoluments or privileges from the community.[a]

---

[a]This clause may serve as the source of the weakest form of uniformity requirement in taxation, certainly not prohibiting classification. Connecticut does not really deal with the subject of taxation in its constitution.

Delaware Constitution (1897)

Art. VIII, § 1. [Uniformity of taxes; assessment and taxation of land devoted to agriculture and forest use; collection under general laws; exemption for public welfare purposes]

All taxes shall be uniform upon the same class of subjects within the territorial limits of the authority levying the tax, except as otherwise permitted herein, and shall be levied and collected under general laws passed by the General Assembly. County Councils of New Castle and Sussex Counties and the Levy Court of Kent County are hereby authorized to exempt from county taxation such property in their respective counties as in their opinion will best promote the public welfare. The county property tax exemption power created by this section shall be exclusive as to such property as is located within the respective counties with respect to real property located within the boundaries of any incorporated municipality; the authority to exempt such property from municipal property tax shall be exercised by the respective incorporated municipality; when in the opinion of the said municipality it will best promote the public welfare.

The legislature shall enact laws to provide that the value of land which is determined by the assessing officer of the taxing jurisdiction to be actively devoted to agriculture use and to have been so devoted for at least the two successive years immediately preceding the tax year in issue, shall, for local tax purposes, on application of the owner, be that value which such land has for agricultural use.

Any such laws shall provide that when land which has been valued in this manner for local tax purposes is applied to a use other than for agriculture, it shall be subject to additional taxes in an amount equal to the difference, if any, between the taxes paid or payable on the basis of the valuation and the assessment authorized hereunder and the taxes that would have been paid or payable had the land been valued and assessed as otherwise provided in this Constitution, in the current year and in such of the tax years immediately preceding, not less than two such years in which the land was valued as herein authorized.

Such laws shall also provide for the assessment and collection of any additional taxes levied thereupon and shall include such other provisions as shall be necessary to carry out the provisions of this amendment.

Art. VIII, § 7. [Real estate assessments; inclusion of values]

In all assessments of the value of real estate for taxation, the value of the land and the value of the buildings and improvements thereon shall be included. And in all assessments of the rental value of real estate for taxation, the rental value of the land and the rental value of the buildings and the improvements thereon shall be included. The foregoing provisions of this section shall apply to all assessments of the value of real estate or of the rental value thereof for taxation for State, county, hundred, school, municipal or other public purposes.

Art. VIII, § 9. [Retroactive increase of taxation of personal income] Any law which shall have the effect of increasing the rates of taxation on personal income for any year of part thereof prior to the date of the enactment thereof, or for any year or years prior to the year in which the law is enacted, shall be void.

Art. X, § 3. . . . all real or personal property used for school purposes, where the tuition is free, shall be exempt from taxation and assessment for public purposes.

Florida Constitution (1968)

Art. VII, § 1. (a) No tax shall be levied except in pursuance of law. No state ad valorem taxes shall be levied upon real estate or tangible personal property. All other forms of taxation shall be preempted to the state except as provided by general law.

(b) ... mobile homes, as defined by law, shall be subject to a license tax for their operation in the amounts and for the purposes prescribed by law, but shall not be subject to ad valorem taxes.

. . . .

Art. VII, § 2. All ad valorem taxation shall be at a uniform rate within each taxing unit, except the taxes on intangible personal property may be at different rates but shall never exceed two mills on the dollar of assessed value; provided as to any obligations secured by mortgage, deed of trust, or other lien on real estate wherever located, an intangible tax of not more than two mills on the dollar may be levied by law to be in lieu of all other intangible assessments on such obligations.

Art. VII, § 3. (a) All property owned by a municipality and used exclusively by it for municipal or public purposes shall be exempt from taxation. A municipality, owning property outside the municipality, may be required by general law to make payment to the taxing unit in which the property is located. Such portions of property as are used predominantly for educational, literary, scientific, religious or charitable purposes may be exempted by general law from taxation.

. . . .

Art. VII, § 4. By general law regulations shall be prescribed which shall secure a just valuation of all property for ad valorem taxation, provided:

(a) Agricultural land or land used exclusively for non-commercial recreational purposes may be classified by general law and assessed solely on the basis of character or use.

Art. VII, § 5. Estate, inheritance and income taxes

(a) **Natural Persons.** No tax upon estates or inheritances or upon the income of natural persons who are residents or citizens of the state shall be levied by the state, or under its authority, in excess of the aggregate of amounts which may be allowed to be credited upon or deducted from any similar tax levied by the United States or any state.

(b) **Others.** No tax upon the income of residents and citizens other than natural persons shall be levied by the state, or under its authority, in excess of 5% of net income, as defined by law, or at such greater rate as is authorized by a three-fifths (3/5) vote of the membership of each house of the legislature or as will provide for the state the maximum amount which may be allowed to be credited against income taxes levied by the United States and other states. There shall be exempt from taxation not of the excess of net income subject to less than five thousand dollars ($5,000) tax over the maximum amount allowed to be credited against income taxes levied by the United States and other states.

Art. VII, § 9. Local taxes

(a) Counties, school districts, and municipalities shall, and special districts may, be authorized by law to levy ad valorem taxes and may be authorized by general law to levy other taxes, for their respective purposes, except ad valorem taxes on intangible personal property and taxes prohibited by this constitution.

(b) Ad valorem taxes, exclusive of taxes levied for the payment of bonds and taxes levied for periods not longer than two years when authorized by vote of the electors who are the owners of freeholds therein not wholly exempt from taxation, shall not be levied in excess of the following millages upon the assessed value of real estate and tangible personal property: for all county purposes, ten mills; for all municipal purposes, ten mills; for all school purposes, ten mills; for water management purposes for the northwest portion of the state lying west of the line between ranges two and three east, 0.05 mill; for water management purposes for the remaining portions of the state, 1.0 mill; and for all other special districts a millage authorized by law approved by vote of the electors who are owners of freeholds therein not wholly exempt from taxation. A county furnishing municipal services may, to the extent authorized by law, levy additional taxes within the limits fixed for municipal purposes.

Art. VIII, § 1. (h) Taxes; limitation. Property situated within municipalities shall not be subject to taxation for services rendered by the county exclusively for the benefit of the property or residents in unincorporated areas.

Georgia Constitution (1976)

Art. VII, § I, Para. I. *Taxation, a Sovereign Right.* The right of taxation is a sovereign right—inalienable, indestructible—is the life of the State, and rightfully belongs to the people in all republican governments, and neither the General Assembly, nor any, nor all other departments of the Government established by this Constitution, shall ever have the authority to irrevocably give, grant, limit, or restrain this right; and all laws, grants, contracts, and all other acts, whatsoever, by said government, or any department thereof, to affect any of these purposes, shall be, and are hereby, declared to be null and void, for every purpose whatsoever, and said right of taxation shall always be under the complete control of, and revocable by, the State, notwithstanding any gift, grant or contract, whatsoever, by the General Assembly.

The power to tax corporations and corporate property, shall not be surrendered or suspended by any contract, or grant to which the State shall be a party.

Art. VII, § I, Para. II. *Taxing Power Limited.* The levy of taxes on property from any one year by the General Assembly for all purposes, except to provide for repelling invasions, suppressing insurrections, or defending the State in time of war, shall not exceed one-fourth (¼) mill on each dollar of the value of the property taxable in the State. . . .

Art. VII, § I, Para. III. *Uniformity; Classification of Property.* All taxes shall be levied and collected under general laws and for public purposes only. All taxation shall be uniform upon the same class of subjects within the territorial limits of the authority levying the tax. Classes of subjects for taxation of property shall consist of tangible property and one or more classes of intangible personal property including money. The General Assembly shall have the power to classify property including money for taxation, and to adopt different rates and different methods for different classes of such property.

. . . .

Notwithstanding anything to the contrary contained in this paragraph, the General Assembly shall be authorized to enact legislation treating any and all mobile homes, other than those mobile homes which qualify the owner thereof for the homestead property tax exemption under Georgia law, as a separate class of property from other classes of tangible property for ad valorem tax purposes, and to adopt different rates, methods or assessment dates for the taxation of such property and to enact legislation consistent herewith to prevent any person, firm or corporation from escaping payment of their fair share of ad valorem taxes on said mobile homes.

The General Assembly may provide for a different method and time of returns, assessments, payment and collection of ad valorem taxes, of public utilities, but not a greater basis of value or at a higher rate of taxation than other properties.

Art. VII, § I, Para. IV. *Exemptions From Taxation.* The General Assembly may, by law, exempt from taxation all public property; places of religious worship or burial and all property owned by religious groups used only for residential purposes and from which no income is derived; all institutions of purely public charity . . . all buildings erected for and used as a college, incorporated academy or other seminary of learning, and also all funds or property held or used as endowment by such colleges, incorporated academies or seminaries of learning, provided the same is not invested in real estate; and provided, further, that said exemptions shall only apply to such colleges, incorporated academies or other seminaries of learning as are open to the general public; the real and personal estate of any public library, and that of any other literary association, used by or connected with such library . . . this exemption shall not apply to real estate or buildings other than those used for the operation of such institution and which is rented, leased or otherwise used for the primary purpose of securing an income thereon; and also provided that such donations of property shall not be predicated upon an agreement, contract or otherwise that the donor or donors shall receive or retain any part of the net or gross income of the property. The General Assembly shall further have power to exempt from taxation farm products, including baled cotton, grown in this State and remaining in the hands of the producer, but not longer than for the year next after their production.

. . . .

The homestead of each resident of Georgia actually occupied by the owner as a residence and homestead, and only so long as actually occupied by the owner primarily as such, but not to exceed $2,000.00 of its value, is hereby exempted from all ad valorem taxation for State, County and school purposes, except taxes levied by municipalities for school purposes and except to pay interest on and retire bonded indebtedness, provided, however, should the owner of a dwelling house on a farm, who is already entitled to homestead exemption, participate in the program of rural housing and obtain a new house under contract with the local housing authority, he shall be entitled to receive the same homestead exemption as allowed before making such contract. The General Assembly may from time to time lower said exemption to not less than $1,250.00. The value of all property in excess of the foregoing exemptions shall remain subject to taxation. Said exemptions shall be returned and claimed in such manner as prescribed by the General Assembly. The exemption herein provided for shall not apply to taxes levied by municipalities.

. . . .

Each disabled veteran, as hereinafter defined, who is a citizen and resident of Georgia, is hereby granted an exemption of $12,500.00[a] on his homestead, which he owns and which he actually occupies as a residence and homestead, such exemption being from all ad valorem taxation for State, county, municipal and school purposes. The value of all property in excess of the above exempted amount shall remain subject to taxation. . . .

Each person who is sixty-five (65) years of age or over is hereby granted an exemption from all State and county ad valorem taxes in the amount of $4,000.00 on a homestead owned and occupied by him as a residence of his net income, together with the net income of his spouse who also occupies and resides at such homestead, as net income is defined by Georgia law, from all sources, except as hereinafter provided, does not exceed $4,000.00 for the immediately preceding taxable year for income tax purposes. . . . The value of the residence in excess of the above exempted amount shall remain subject to taxation. . . .

The General Assembly shall have the authority to provide for the exemption from any and all taxation any facilities which shall be installed or constructed for the primary purpose of eliminating or reducing air or water pollution. . . .

The governing authority of any county or municipality may exempt from ad valorem taxation, including all such taxes levied for State, county, municipal, or school purposes, all of the value of certain tangible property used in a solar energy heating or cooling system, and all the value of certain tangible property consisting only of machinery and equipment directly used in the manufacture of solar energy heating or cooling systems. . . .

The General Assembly shall be authorized to exempt from ad valorem taxation property of nonprofit hospitals used in connection with their operation. . . .

The General Assembly shall be authorized to exempt from ad valorem taxation property of nonprofit homes for the aged used in connection with their operation. . . .

The homestead of each resident of each independent school district who is 62 years of age or over and who does not have an income from all sources, including the income from all sources of all members of the family residing within said homestead, exceeding $6,000.00 per annum, may be exempt by law from all ad valorem taxation for educational purposes levied for and in behalf of such school system. . . .

[Preceding exemption provisions also apply to county school districts.]

. . . .

In order to encourage and enhance overall economic development, increase employment, promote agribusiness, and to provide incentives for the location of new and expanding manufacturing and processing facilities, harvested agricultural products which have a planting-to-harvest cycle of 12 months or less, which

---

[a] A November 1978 amendment increased this amount to $25,000.

are customarily cured and aged for a period in excess of one year after harvesting, and before manufacturing, and which are held in this State for manufacturing or processing purposes, shall be exempt from all ad valorem taxation. . . .

All laws exempting property from taxation, other than the property herein enumerated, shall be void.

Art. VII, § I, Para. V. *Revocation of Tax Exemptions.* All exemptions from taxation heretofore granted in corporate charters are declared to be henceforth null and void.

Art. VII, § II, Para. I. *Taxation, How and For What Purposes Exercised.* The powers of taxation over the whole State shall be exercised by the General Assembly for the following purposes only:

1. For the support of the State Government and the public institutions.
2. For educational purposes.
3. [Pay public debt]
4. [Defend State]
5. [Pay Confederate pensions]
6. To construct and maintain State buildings and a system of State highways, airports, and docks.
7. [Pay various welfare benefits]
8. [Social Security, etc. purposes]
9. To advertise and promote the agricultural, industrial, historic, recreational and natural resources of the State of Georgia.
10. For public health purposes.
11. Public transportation of passengers for hire . . . provided, however, that the State of Georgia shall not provide more than 10 per cent of the total cost, either directly or indirectly. . . .
12. For school lunch purposes.
13. [School expenditures]

Art. VII, § II, Para. II. Any other provision of this Constitution notwithstanding, the General Assembly may provide for the promotion of the production . . . of any one or all of the agricultural products including, but not limited to . . . timber and timber products, fish and sea food, and the products of the farms and forests of this State . . . . The General Assembly may provide that such a program including provisions for quality and/or product control may be instituted, continued or terminated by a specified vote of the producers of the product or products affected participating in a referendum submitting such proposal for their approval. The General Assembly may create instrumentalities, public corporations, authorities and commissions, to administer such programs, and may provide a means of financing any such promotion by authorizing such bodies to impose, raise, lower or repeal assessments, fees and other charges upon the sale or processing of the affected products . . . . The uniformity requirement of this

Constitution shall be satisfied by the application of the program upon the affected products.

Art. VII, § II, Para. IV. *Grants to Municipalities.* Notwithstanding any other provisions of this Constitution, the General Assembly is hereby authorized to provide by law for the granting of State funds to the municipalities of Georgia, in such manner and form and under such procedure as the General Assembly may prescribe. The General Assembly is also authorized but not directed, to provide the purpose or purposes for which such funds may be expended by the municipalities. The General Assembly is hereby authorized to exercise the power of taxation over the entire State in order to carry out the provisions of this Paragraph.

Art. VII, § II, Para. V. *Industrial Development Commission.* The General Assembly shall have the power to create an Industrial Development Commission to make loans, to be secured by second mortgages, to such industrial development agencies as the Industrial Development Commission may select. . . . The powers of taxation may be exercised through the General Assembly in order to implement and carry out the purposes for which said Commission is to be created.

Art. VIII, § VII, Para. I. *Local Taxation for Education.* The fiscal authority of each county shall annually levy a school tax for the support and maintenance of education, not greater than twenty mills per dollar as certified to it by the county board of education, upon the assessed value of all taxable property within the county located outside any independent school system or area school district therein. . . .

Art. IX, § IV, Para. II. *Supplementary Powers.* In addition to and supplementary of any powers now conferred upon and possessed by any county, municipality, or any combination thereof, any county, any municipality and any combination of any such political subdivisions may exercise the following powers and provide the following services:
   (1) Police and fire protection.
   (2) Garbage and solid waste collection and disposal.
   (3) Public health facilities and services. . . .
   (4) Street and road construction and maintenance. . . .
   (5) Parks, recreational areas, programs and facilities.
   (6) Storm water and sewage collection and disposal systems.
   (7) . . . purification and distribution of water.
   (8) Public housing.
   (9) Urban redevelopment programs.
   (10) Public transportation system.
   (11) Libraries.
   (12) Terminal and dock facilities and parking facilities.

(13) Building, housing, plumbing and electrical codes.
(14) Air Pollution Control.
(15) Planning and zoning. . . .

. . . the powers of taxation and assessment may be exercised by any county, municipality or any combination thereof, or within any such district, for the above powers and in order to provide such services.

Art. IX, § IV, Para. III. *Taxing Power and Contributions of Counties, Cities and Political Division Restricted.* The General Assembly shall not authorize any county, municipal corporation or political division of this State, through taxation, contribution or otherwise, to become a stockholder in any company, corporation or association, or to appropriate money for, or to loan its credit to any corporation, company, association, institution or individual except for purely charitable purposes. This restriction shall not operate to prevent the support of schools by municipal corporations within their respective limits.

Art. IX, § V, Para. I. *Power of County Government.* The General Assembly may authorize any county to exercise the power of taxation for any public purpose as authorized by general law or by this Constitution, and unless otherwise provided by this Constitution or by law, no levy need state the particular purposes for which the same was made nor shall any taxes collected be allocated for any particular purpose, unless expressly so provided by the General Assembly or this Constitution.

Art. IX, § V, Para. II. *Purposes of Taxation.* In addition to such other powers and authority as may be conferred upon any county by this Constitution or by the General Assembly, counties are hereby authorized to exercise the power of taxation for the following purposes which are hereby declared to be public purposes, and expend funds raised by the exercise of said powers for said purposes and such other public purposes as may be authorized by the General Assembly:

1. Pay the expenses of administration of the county government.
2. [Public Works]
3. [Courts]
4. [Public Health]
5. [County Police]
6. [Medical or other care for indigent]
7. [County Agricultural Agents]
8. [Welfare Benefits]
9. Provide fire protection for forest lands and conserve natural resources.
10. [Provide insurance, retirement and pension benefits; coverage under F.O.A.S.I., etc.]
11. Establish and maintain a recreation system.

12. [Paying of any debt of the county]
13. [Reserves for Public Improvements]
14. [Public Education]

Hawaii Constitution
(1950. Rev. 1968)[a]

Art. VI, § 1. The power of taxation shall never be surrendered, suspended or contracted away.

Art.VI, § 2. No tax shall be levied or appropriation of public money or property made, nor shall the public credit be used, directly or indirectly, except for a public purpose. . . .

Art. VII, § 3. The taxing power shall be reserved to the State except so much thereof as may be delegated by the legislature to the political subdivisions, and the legislature shall have the power to apportion state revenues among the several political subdivisions.

Art. VII, § 5. This article shall not limit the power of the legislature to enact laws of state-wide concern.

Art. XIV, § 10. No taxes shall be imposed by the State upon any lands or other property now owned or hereafter acquired by the United States, except as the same shall become taxable by reason of disposition thereof by the United States or by reason of the consent of the United States to such taxation.

---

[a] Hawaii's constitution was revised November 1978. See appendix B. Provisions shown as art. VI, § 1 art. VI, § 2, art. VII, and art. XIV have been renumbered as art. VII, § 1, art. VII, § 4, art. VIII, and art. XVI, respectively.

Idaho Constitution (1890)

Art. III, § 19. *Local and special laws prohibited.*—The legislature shall not pass local or special laws in any of the following enumerated cases, that is to say:

. . . .

For the assessment and collection of taxes.

. . . .

Extending the time for collection of taxes.

. . . .

Exempting property from taxation.

. . . .

Art. VII, § 2. *Revenue to be provided by taxation.*—The legislature shall provide such revenue as may be needful, by levying a tax by valuation, so that every person or corporation shall pay a tax in proportion to the value of his, her, or its property, except as in this article hereinafter otherwise provided. The legislature may also impose a license tax, both upon natural persons and upon corporations, other than municipal, doing business in this state; also a per capita tax: provided, the legislature may exempt a limited amount of improvements upon land from taxation.

Art. VII, § 3. *Property to be defined and classified.*—The word "property" as herein used shall be defined and classified by law.

Art. VII, § 4. *Public property exempt from taxation.*—The property of the United States, except when taxation thereof is authorized by the United States, the state, counties, towns, cities, villages, school districts, and other municipal corporations and public libraries shall be exempt from taxation.

Art. VII, § 5. *Taxes to be uniform—Exemptions.*—All taxes shall be uniform upon the same class of subjects within the territorial limits, of the authority levying the tax, and shall be levied and collected under general laws, which shall prescribe such regulations as shall secure a just valuation for taxation of all property, real and personal: provided, that the legislature may allow such exemptions from taxation from time to time as shall seem necessary and just, and all existing exemptions provided by the laws of the territory, shall continue until changed by the legislature of the state: provided further, that duplicate taxation of property for the same purpose during the same year, is hereby prohibited.

Art. VII, § 6. *Municipal corporations to impose their own taxes.*—The legislature shall not impose taxes for the purpose of any county, city, town, or other municipal corporation, but may by law invest in the corporate authorities thereof, respectively, the power to assess and collect taxes for all purposes of such corporation.

Art. VII, § 7. *State taxes to be paid in full.* —All taxes levied for state purposes shall be paid into the state treasury, and no county, city, town, or other municipal corporation, the inhabitants thereof, nor the property therein, shall be released or discharged from their or its proportionate share of taxes to be levied for state purposes.

Art. VII, § 8. *Corporate property must be taxed.* —The power to tax corporations or corporate property, both real and personal, shall never be relinquished or suspended, and all corporations in this state or doing business therein, shall be subject to taxation for state, county, school, municipal, and other purposes, on real and personal property owned or used by them, and not by this constitution exempted from taxation within the territorial limits of the authority levying the tax.

Art. VII, § 9. *Maximum rate of taxation.* —The rate of taxation of real and personal property for state purposes shall never exceed ten mills on each dollar of assessed valuation, unless a proposition to increase such rate, specifying the rate proposed and the time during which the same shall be levied, shall have been submitted to the people at a general election, and shall have received a majority of all the votes cast for and against it at such election.

Art. XXI, § 19. . . .lands belonging to citizens of the United States, residing without the said state of Idaho, shall never be taxed at a higher rate than the lands belonging to the residents thereof. . .no taxes shall be imposed by the state on lands or property therein belonging to, or which may hereafter be purchased by, the United States, or reserved for its use. . . .

Illinois Constitution (1970)

Art. VII, § 6. POWERS OF HOME RULE UNITS

(e) A home rule unit shall have only the power that the General Assembly may provide by law. . . (2) to license for revenue or impose taxes upon or measured by income or earnings or upon occupations. . . .

(g) The General Assembly by a law approved by the vote of three-fifths of the members elected to each house may deny or limit the power to tax and any other power or function of a home rule unit not exercised or performed by the State. . . .

(l) The General Assembly may not deny or limit the power of home rule units (1) to make local improvements by special assessment and to exercise this power jointly with other counties and municipalities, and other classes of units of local government having that power on the effective date of this Constitution unless that power is subsequently denied by law to any such other units of local government or (2) to levy or impose additional taxes upon areas within their boundaries in the manner provided by law for the provision of special services to those areas and for the payment of debt incurred in order to provide those special services.

. . . .

Art. VII, § 7. COUNTIES AND MUNICIPALITIES OTHER THAN HOME RULE UNITS

Counties and municipalities which are not home rule units shall have only powers granted to them by law and the powers (1) to make local improvements by special assessment and to exercise this power jointly with other counties and municipalities, and other classes of units of local government having that power on the effective date of this Constitution unless that power is subsequently denied by law to any such other units of local government . . . and (6) to levy or impose additional taxes upon areas within their boundaries in the manner provided by law for the provision of special services to those areas and for the payment of debt incurred in order to provide those special services.

Art. VII, § 8. Townships, school districts special districts and units, designated by law as units of local government, which exercise limited governmental powers or powers in respect to limited governmental subjects shall have only powers granted by law. . . .

Art. IX, § 1. STATE REVENUE POWER

The General Assembly has the exclusive power to raise revenue by law except as limited or otherwise provided in this Constitution. The power of taxation shall not be surrendered, suspended, or contracted away.

Art. IX, § 2. NON-PROPERTY TAXES—CLASSIFICATION, EXEMPTIONS, DEDUCTIONS, ALLOWANCES AND CREDITS

In any law classifying the subjects or objects of non-property taxes or fees, the classes shall be reasonable and the subjects and objects within each class shall be taxed uniformly. Exemptions, deductions, credits, refunds and other allowances shall be reasonable.

Art. IX, § 3. LIMITATIONS ON INCOME TAXATION

(a) A tax on or measured by income shall be at a non-graduated rate. At any one time there may be no more than one such tax imposed by the State for State purposes on individuals and one such tax so imposed on corporations. In any such tax imposed upon corporations the rate shall not exceed the rate imposed on individuals by more than a ratio of 8 to 5.

. . . .

Art. IX, § 4. REAL PROPERTY TAXATION

(a) Except as otherwise provided in this Section, taxes upon real property shall be levied uniformly by valuation ascertained as the General Assembly shall provide by law.

(b) Subject to such limitations as the General Assembly may hereafter prescribe by law, counties with a population of more than 200,000 may classify or to continue to classify real property for purposes of taxation. Any such classification shall be reasonable and assessments shall be uniform within each class. The level of assessment or rate of tax of the highest class in a county shall not exceed two and one-half times the level of assessment or rate of tax of the lowest class in that county. Real property used in farming in a county shall not be assessed at a higher level of assessment than single family residential real property in that county.

. . . .

Art. IX, § 5. PERSONAL PROPERTY TAXATION

(a) The General Assembly by law may classify personal property for purposes of taxation by valuation, abolish such taxes on any or all classes and authorize the levy of taxes in lieu of the taxation of personal property by valuation.

(b) Any ad valorem personal property tax abolished on or before the effective date of this Constitution shall not be reinstated.

(c) On or before January 1, 1979, the General Assembly by law shall abolish all ad valorem personal property taxes and concurrently therewith and thereafter shall replace all revenue lost by units of local government and school districts as a result of the abolition of ad valorem personal property taxes subsequent to January 2, 1971. Such revenue shall be replaced by imposing statewide taxes, other than ad valorem taxes on real estate, solely on those classes relieved of the burden of paying ad valorem personal property taxes because of the abolition of such taxes subsequent to January 2, 1971. If any taxes imposed for such replacement purposes are taxes on or measured by income, such replacement taxes shall not be considered for purposes of the limitations of one tax and the ratio of 8 to 5 set forth in Section 3(a) of this Article.

Art. IX, § 6. EXEMPTIONS FROM PROPERTY TAXATION

The General Assembly by law may exempt from taxation only the property of the State, units of local government and school districts and property used exclusively for agricultural and horticultural societies, and for school, religious, cemetery and charitable purposes. The General Assembly by law may grant homestead exemptions or rent credits.

Art. IX, § 7. OVERLAPPING TAXING DISTRICTS

The General Assembly may provide by law for fair apportionment of the burden of taxation of property situated in taxing districts that lie in more than one county.

Indiana Constitution (1851)

Art. IV, § 22. The General Assembly shall not pass local or special laws, in any of the fellowing [*sic*] enumerated cases, that is to say:

. . . .

For the assessment and collection of taxes for State, county, township, or road purposes. . . .

Art. X, § 1. [Property assessment and taxation]
(a) The General Assembly shall provide, by law, for a uniform and equal rate of property assessment and taxation and shall prescribe regulations to secure a just valuation for taxation of all property, both real and personal. The General Assembly may exempt from property taxation any property in any of the following classes:

(1) Property being used for municipal, educational, literary, scientific, religious or charitable purposes;

(2) Tangible personal property other than property being held for sale in the ordinary course of a trade or business, property being held, used or consumed in connection with the production of income, or property being held as an investment;

(3) Intangible personal property.

(b) The General Assembly may exempt any . . . mobile homes . . . or similar property, provided that an excise tax in lieu of the property tax is substituted therefor.

Art. X, § 8. [Income tax; levy and collection authorized]
The general assembly may levy and collect a tax upon income, from whatever source derived, at such rates, in such manner, and with such exemptions as may be prescribed by law.

Iowa Constitution (1857)

Art. III, § 30. The General Assembly shall not pass local or special laws in the following cases: For the assessment and collection of taxes for State, County, or road purposes. . . .

Art. VII, § 7. [Tax imposed distinctly stated.] Every law which imposes, continues, or revives a tax, shall distinctly state the tax, and the object to which it is to be applied; and it shall not be sufficient to refer to any other law to fix such tax or object.

Art. VIII, § 2. [Taxation of corporations.] The property of all corporations for pecuniary profit, shall be subject to taxation, the same as that of individuals.

Art. IX, Pt. 1, § 10. The Board [of Education] shall have no power to levy taxes. . . .

Amend. 2 of 1968. Art. III. *Municipal home rule.* Municipal corporations are granted home rule power and authority, not inconsistent with the laws of the General Assembly, to determine their local affairs and government, except that they shall not have power to levy any tax unless expressly authorized by the General Assembly.

The rule or proposition of law that a municipal corporation possesses and can exercise only those powers granted in express words is not a part of the law of this state.

Kansas Constitution (1861)

Art. 6, § 6. *(a)* The legislature may levy a permanent tax for the use and benefit of state institutions of higher education. . . .

Art. 7, § 5. Unemployment compensation; old-age benefits; taxation.
. . . No direct ad valorem tax shall be laid on real or personal property for such purposes.

Art. 7, § 6. Tax levy for certain institutions. The legislature may levy a permanent tax for the creation of a building fund for [various welfare] institutions. . . .

Art. 11, § 2. Taxation of incomes. The state shall have power to levy and collect taxes on incomes from whatever source derived, which taxes may be graduated and progressive.

Art. 11, § 5. Object of tax. No tax shall be levied except in pursuance of a law, which shall distinctly state the object of the same; to which object only such tax shall be applied.

Art. 11, § 9. The state . . . may adopt, construct, reconstruct and maintain a state system of highways, but no general property tax shall ever be laid nor general obligation bonds issued by the state for such highways. . . .

Art. 11, § 10. Special taxes for highway purposes. The state shall have power to levy special taxes, for road and highway purposes, on motor vehicles and on motor fuels.

Art. 12, § 5. *(b)* **Cities empowered to determine their local affairs.** Cities are hereby empowered to determine their local affairs and government including the levying of taxes, excises, fees, charges and other exactions except when and as the levying of any tax, excise, fee, charge or other exaction is limited or prohibited by enactment of the legislature applicable uniformly to all cities of the same class: Provided, That the legislature may establish not to exceed four classes of cities for the purpose of imposing all such limitations or prohibitions. . . .

Amend. 1974, Art. 2, § 17. Uniform operation of laws of a general nature. All laws of a general nature shall have a uniform operation throughout the state: Provided, The legislature may designate areas in counties that have become urban in character as "urban areas" and enact special laws giving to any one or more of such counties or urban areas such powers of local government and consolidation of local government as the legislature may deem proper.

Kansas Constitution

Amend. 1974, Art. 11, § 1. System of taxation; classifications; exemption. The legislature shall provide for a uniform and equal rate of assessment and taxation, except that the legislature may provide for the classification and the taxation uniformly as to class of motor vehicles, mineral products, money, mortgages, notes and other evidence of debt or may exempt any of such classes of property from property taxation and impose taxes upon another basis in lieu thereof. All property used exclusively for state, county, municipal, literary, educational, scientific, religious, benevolent and charitable purposes, and all household goods and personal effects not used for the production of income, shall be exempted from property taxation.

Amend. 1974, Art. 11, § 12. Assessment and taxation of land devoted to agricultural use. Land devoted to agricultural use may be defined by law and valued for ad valorem tax purposes upon the basis of its agricultural income or agricultural productivity, actual or potential, and when so valued such land shall be assessed at the same percent of value and taxed at the same rate as real property subject to the provisions of section 1 of this article. The legislature may, if land devoted to agricultural use changes from such use, provide for the recoupment of a part or all of the difference between the amount of the ad valorem taxes levied upon such land during a part or all of the period in which it was valued in accordance with the provisions of this section and the amount of ad valorem taxes which would have been levied upon such land during such period had it not been in agricultural use and had it been valued, assessed and taxed in accordance with section 1 of this article.

Kentucky Constitution (1891)

Bill of Rights, § 3. . . . no property shall be exempt from taxation except as provided in this Constitution, and every grant of a franchise, privilege or exemption, shall remain subject to revocation, alteration or amendment.

§ 59. [Local and special legislation.] The General Assembly shall not pass local or special acts concerning any of the following subjects, or for any of the following purposes, namely:

. . . .

Fifteenth: To authorize or to regulate the levy, the assessment or the collection of taxes, or to give any indulgence or discharge to any assessor or collector of taxes, or to his sureties.

. . . .

§ 157. . . . The tax rate of cities, towns, counties, taxing districts and other municipalities, for other than school purposes, shall not at any time, exceed the following rates upon the value of the taxable property therein, viz.: For all towns or cities having a population of fifteen thousand or more, one dollar and fifty cents on the hundred dollars; for all towns or cities having less than fifteen thousand and not less than ten thousand, one dollar on the hundred dollars; for all towns or cities having less than ten thousand, seventy-five cents on the hundred dollars; and for counties and taxing districts, fifty cents on the hundred dollars. . . .

§ 170. [Property exempt from taxation — Cities may exempt factories for five years.] — There shall be exempt from taxation public property used for public purposes; places actually used for religious worship, with the grounds attached thereto and used and appurtenant to the house of worship, not exceeding one half acre in cities or towns, and not exceeding two acres in the country; places of burial not held for private or corporate profit, institutions of purely public charity, and institutions of education not used or employed for gain by any person or corporation, and the income of which is devoted solely to the cause of education, public libraries, their endowments, and the income of such property as is used exclusively for their maintenance; all parsonages or residences owned by any religious society, and occupied as a home, or residences owned by any religious society, and occupied as a home, and for no other purpose, by the minister of any religion, with not exceeding one half acre of ground in towns and cities and two acres of ground in the country appurtenant thereto; household goods of a person used in his home; crops grown in the year in which the assessment is made, and in the hands of the producer; and real property maintained as the permanent residence of the owner, who is sixty-five years of age or older, up to the assessed valuation of sixty-five hundred dollars on said residence

Kentucky Constitution

and contiguous real property, except for assessment for special benefits. The real property may be held by legal or equitable title, by the entireties, jointly, in common, as a condominium, or indirectly by the stock ownership or membership representing the owner's or member's proprietary interest in a corporation owning a fee or a leasehold initially in excess of ninety-eight years. The exemption shall apply only to the value of the real property assessable to the owner or, in case of ownership through stock or membership in a corporation, the value of the proportion which his interest in the corporation bears to the assessed value of the property. All laws exempting or omitting property from taxation other than the property above mentioned shall be void. The general assembly may authorize any incorporated city or town to exempt manufacturing establishments from municipal taxation, for a period not exceeding five years, as an inducement to their location.

§ 171. ... The General Assembly shall provide by law an annual tax, which, with other resources, shall be sufficient to defray the estimated expenses of the Commonwealth for each fiscal year. Taxes shall be levied and collected for public purposes only and shall be uniform upon all property of the same class subject to taxation within the territorial limits of the authority levying the tax; and all taxes shall be levied and collected by general laws.

The General Assembly shall have power to divide property into classes and to determine what class or classes of property shall be subject to local taxation. ...

§ 172. All property, not exempted from taxation by this Constitution, shall be assessed for taxation at its fair cash value, estimated at the price it would bring at a fair voluntary sale. ...

§ 172A. [**Assessment of farm land according to value for farm purposes.**] Notwithstanding contrary provisions of Sections 171, 172 or 174 of this Constitution —

The General Assembly shall provide by general law for the assessment for ad valorem tax purposes of agricultural and horticultural land according to the land's value for agricultural or horticultural use. The General Assembly may provide that any change in land use from agricultural or horticultural to another use shall require the levy of an additional tax not to exceed the additional amount that would have been owing had the land been assessed under Section 172 of this Constitution for the current year and the two next preceding years.

The General Assembly may provide for reasonable differences in the rate of ad valorem taxation within different areas of the same taxing districts on that class of property which includes the surface of the land. Those differences shall relate directly to differences between non-revenue-producing governmental services and benefits giving land urban character which are furnished in one or several areas in contrast to other areas of the taxing district.

§ 174. [**Property to be taxed according to value, whether corporate or individual; income, license and franchise taxes.**] All property, whether owned by natural persons or corporations, shall be taxed in proportion to its value, unless exempted by this Constitution; and all corporate property shall pay the same rate of taxation paid by individual property. Nothing in this Constitution shall be construed to prevent the General Assembly from providing for taxation based on income, licenses or franchises.

§ 175. [**Power to tax property not to be surrendered.**] The power to tax property shall not be surrendered or suspended by any contract or grant to which the Commonwealth shall be a party.

§ 181. [**General Assembly may not levy tax for political subdivision, but may confer power; license and excise taxes; city taxes in lieu of ad valorem taxes.**] The General Assembly shall not impose taxes for the purposes of any county, city, town or other municipal corporation, but may, by general laws, confer on the proper authorities thereof, respectively, the power to assess and collect such taxes. The General Assembly may, by general laws only, provide for the payment of license fees on franchises, stock used for breeding purposes, the various trades, occupations and professions, or a special or excise tax; and may, by general laws, delegate the power to counties, towns, cities and other municipal corporations, to impose and collect license fees on stock used for breeding purposes, on franchises, trades, occupations and professions. And the General Assembly may, by general laws only, authorize cities or towns of any class to provide for taxation for municipal purposes on personal property, tangible and intangible, based on income, licenses or franchises, in lieu of an ad valorem tax thereon: Provided, Cities of the first class shall not be authorized to omit the imposition of an ad valorem tax on such property of any steam railroad, street railway, ferry, bridge, gas, water, heating, telephone, telegraph, electric light or electric power company.

§ 182. [**Railroad taxes; how assessed and collected.**] Nothing in this Constitution shall be construed to prevent the General Assembly from providing by law how railroads and railroad property shall be assessed and how taxes thereon shall be collected. And until otherwise provided, the present law on said subject shall remain in force.

Louisiana Constitution (1974)

Art. III, § 12. [(A) Prohibitions.] Except as otherwise provided in this constitution, the legislature shall not pass a local or special law:

. . . .

(5) Exempting property from taxation; extending the time for the assessment or collection of taxes. . . .

. . . .

Art. VI, § 15. [Local Governmental Subdivisions; Control Over Agencies.] The governing authority of a local governmental subdivision shall have general power over any agency heretofore or hereafter created by it, including, without limitation, the power to abolish the agency and require prior approval of any charge or tax levied or bond issued by the agency.

Art. VI, Pt. II, § 26. The governing authority of a parish may levy annually an ad valorem tax for general purposes not to exceed four mills on the dollar of assessed valuation. . . .

Art. VI, Pt. II, § 27. The governing authority of a municipality may levy annually an ad valorem tax for general purposes not to exceed seven mills on the dollar of assessed valuation. . . .

Art. VI, Pt. II, § 28. The governing authority of a local governmental subdivision may impose an occupational license tax not greater than that imposed by the state. . . .

Art. VI, Pt. II, § 30. A political subdivision may exercise the power of taxation, subject to limitations elsewhere provided by this constitution, under authority granted by the legislature for parish, municipal, and other local purposes, strictly public in their nature. This Section shall not affect similar grants to political subdivisions under self-operative sections of this constitution.

Art. VI, Pt. II, § 32. For the purpose of acquiring, constructing, improving, maintaining or operating any work of public improvement, a political subdivision may levy special taxes when authorized by a majority of the electors in the political subdivision who vote thereon in an election held for that purpose.

Art. VI, Pt. II, § 36. [Local Improvements Assessments. (A) Authorization.] The legislature shall provide by general law or by local or special law the procedures by which a political subdivision may levy and collect local or special assessments on real property for the purpose of acquiring, constructing, or improving works of public improvement.

. . . .

Art. VI, Pt. III, § 39. [Levee District Taxes. (A) District Tax; Millage Limit.] For the purpose of constructing and maintaining levees, levee drainage, flood protection, hurricane flood protection, and for all other purposes incidental thereto, the governing authority of a levee district may levy annually a tax not to exceed five mills, except the Board of Levee Commissioners of the Orleans Levee District which may levy annually a tax not to exceed two and one-half mills, on the dollar of the assessed valuation of all taxable property situated within the alluvial portions of the district subject to overflow.
. . . .

Art. VII, Pt. I, § 1. [Power to Tax; Public Purpose.] Except as otherwise provided by this constitution, the power of taxation shall be vested in the legislature, shall never be surrendered, suspended, or contracted away, and shall be exercised for public purposes only.

Art. VII, Pt. I, § 4 [(A) Income Tax.] Equal and uniform taxes may be levied on net incomes, and these taxes may be graduated according to the amount of net income. . . .

 [(B) Severance Tax.] Taxes may be levied on natural resources severed from the soil or water, to be paid proportionately by the owners thereof at the time of severance. Natural resources may be classified for the purpose of taxation. Such taxes may be predicated upon either the quantity or value of the products at the time and place of severance. No further or additional tax or license shall be levied or imposed upon oil, gas, or sulphur leases or rights. No additional value shall be added to the assessment of land by reason of the presence of oil, gas, or sulphur therein or their production therefrom. However, sulphur in place shall be assessed for ad valorem taxation to the person, firm, or corporation having the right to mine or produce the same in the parish where located, at no more than twice the total assessed value of the physical property subject to taxation, excluding the assessed value of sulphur above ground, as is used in sulphur operations in such parish. Likewise, the severance tax shall be the only tax on timber; however, standing timber shall be liable equally with the land on which it stands for ad valorem taxes levied on the land.

 [(C) Severance Tax; Political Subdivisions.] A political subdivision of the state shall not levy a severance tax, income tax, or tax on motor fuel.
. . . .

Art. VII, Pt. II, § 18. [Ad valorem taxes. (A) Assessments.] Property subject to ad valorem taxation shall be listed on the assessment rolls at its assessed valuation, which, except as provided in Paragraph (C), shall be a percentage of its fair market value. The percentage of fair market value shall be uniform throughout the state upon the same class of property.

 [(B) Classification.] The classifications of property subject to ad valorem taxation and the percentage of fair market value applicable to each classification for the purpose of determining assessed valuation are as follows:

Classifications	Percentages
1. Land	10%
2. Improvements for residential purposes	10%
3. Other property	15%

[(C) **Use Value.**] Bona fide agricultural, horticultural, marsh, and timber lands, as defined by general law, shall be assessed for tax purposes at ten percent of use value rather than fair market value. The legislature may provide by law similarly for building of historic architectural importance.

. . . .

Art. VII, Pt. II, § 19. [State Property Taxation; Rate Limitation]
State taxation on property for all purposes shall not exceed an annual rate of five and three-quarter mills on the dollar of assessed valuation.

Art. VII, Pt. II, § 20. [Homestead Exemption. (A) Homeowners.]
(1) The bona fide homestead, consisting of a tract of land or two or more tracts of land with a residence on one tract and a field, pasture, or garden on the other tract or tracts, not exceeding one hundred sixty acres, buildings and appurtenances, whether rural or urban, owned and occupied by any person, shall be exempt from state, parish, and special ad valorem taxes to the extent of three thousand dollars of the assessed valuation.

(2) By law enacted by two-thirds of the elected members of each house, the legislature may increase this homestead exemption to an amount which shall not exceed five thousand dollars of the assessed valuation.

(3) The homestead exemption of veterans of the armed forces of the United States, honorably discharged or separated from such services or other persons who served in said armed forces, as defined by general law, and of persons sixty-five years of age or older shall be five thousand dollars of the assessed valuation.

(4) The homestead exemption shall extend to the surviving spouse or minor children of a deceased owner and shall apply when the homestead is occupied as such and title to it is in either husband or wife but not to more than one homestead owned by the husband or wife.

(5) This exemption shall not extend to municipal taxes. However, the exemption shall apply (a) in Orleans Parish, to state, general city, school, levee, and levee district taxes and (b) to any municipal taxes levied for school purposes.

[(B) **Residential Lessees.**] Notwithstanding any contrary provision in this constitution, the legislature may provide for tax relief to residential lessees in the form of credits or rebates in order to provide equitable tax relief similar to that granted to homeowners through homestead exemptions.

Art. VII, Pt. II, § 21. [Other Property Exemptions] In addition to the homestead exemption provided for in Section 20 of this Article, the following property and no other shall be exempt from ad valorem taxation:

(A) Public lands; other public property used for public purposes.

(B) (1) Property owned by a nonprofit corporation or association organized and operated exclusively for religious, dedicated places of burial, charitable, health, welfare, fraternal, or educational purposes. . . .

(2) property of a bona fide labor organization. . . .

(3) property of an organization such as a lodge or club organized for charitable and fraternal purposes . . . a nonprofit corporation devoted to promoting trade, travel, and commerce, and also property of a trade, business, industry or professional society. . . .

(C) (3) obligations secured by mortgage on property located in Louisiana. . . .

(13) rights-of-way granted to the State Department of Highways. . . .

(F) Notwithstanding any contrary provision of this Section, the State Board of Commerce and Industry or its successor, with the approval of the governor, may enter into contracts for the exemption from ad valorem taxes of a new manufacturing establishment or an addition to an existing manufacturing establishment, on such terms and conditions as the board, with the approval of the governor, deems in the best interest of the state.

The exemption shall be for an initial term of no more than five calendar years, and may be renewed for an additional five years.

Art. IX, § 8. [(A) Forestry; Acreage Taxes.] . . . the legislature . . . may authorize parish governing authorities to levy acreage taxes, not to exceed two cents per acre. . . . The provisions of this constitution exempting homesteads from taxation shall apply to forestry acreage taxes.

Note: A new Article IX, § 9 has been added. See appendix B.

Maine Constitution
(1820. Recod. 1973)

Art. I, § 22. No tax or duty shall be imposed without the consent of the people or of their representatives in the Legislature.

Art. IX, § 8.[a] All taxes upon real and personal estate, assessed by authority of this State, shall be apportioned and assessed equally, according to the just value thereof; but the Legislature shall have power to levy a tax upon intangible personal property at such rate as it deems wise and equitable without regard to the rate applied to other classes of property. Nothing shall prevent the Legislature from providing for the assessment of the following types of real estate wherever situated in accordance with a valuation based upon the current use thereof and in accordance with such conditions as the Legislature may enact:

(1) Farms and agricultural lands, timberland and woodlands;

(2) Open space lands which are used for recreation or the enjoyment of scenic or natural beauty;

(3) Lands used for game management or wildlife sanctuaries.

In implementing the foregoing, the Legislature shall provide that any change of use higher than those set forth above, except when the change is occasioned by a transfer resulting from the exercise or threatened exercise of the power of eminent domain, shall result in the imposition of a minimum penalty equal to the tax which would have been imposed over the 5 years preceding such change of use had such real estate been assessed at its highest and best use, less all taxes paid on said real estate over the preceding 5 years, and interest, upon such reasonable and equitable basis as the Legislature shall determine.

Art. IX, § 9. The Legislature shall never, in any manner, suspend or surrender the power of taxation.

---

[a] Art. IX, § 8 has been rewritten. See appendix B. Also, a new Art. IV, Pt. 3, § 23 has been added.

Maryland Constitution (1867)

Declaration of Rights Art. 14. *No tax, etc. to be levied without consent of legislature.* That no aid, charge, tax, burthen or fees ought to be rated or levied, under any pretense, without the consent of the Legislature.

Declaration of Rights Art. 15. ... the General Assembly shall, by uniform rules, provide for the separate assessment, classification and sub-classification of land, improvements on land and personal property, as it may deem proper; and all taxes thereafter provided to be levied by the State for the support of the general State Government, and by the Counties and by the City of Baltimore for their respective purposes, shall be uniform within each class or sub-class of land, improvements on land and personal property which the respective taxing powers may have directed to be subjected to the tax levy; yet fines, duties or taxes may properly and justly be imposed, or laid with a political view for the good government and benefit of the community.

Art. XI, E, § 5. Notwithstanding any other provision of this Article [Municipal Home Rule Charters], the General Assembly may enact, amend, or repeal local laws placing a maximum limit on the rate at which property taxes may be imposed by any such municipal corporation. ... No such municipal corporation shall levy any type of tax, license fee, franchise tax or fee which was not in effect in such municipal corporation on January 1, 1954, unless it shall receive the express authorization of the General Assembly for such purpose, by a general law which in its terms and its effect applies alike to all municipal corporations in one or more of the classes provided for in ... this Article. ...

Art. XI, G, § 8. Notwithstanding any other provisions of this Article [County Home Rule Charters] the General Assembly has exclusive power to enact, amend, or repeal any local law for a code county which (1) authorizes or places a maximum limit upon the rate of property taxes which may be imposed by the code county. ... Public local laws enacted by the General Assembly under this section prevail over any public local laws enacted by the code county under other sections in this Article.

Art. XI, G, § 9. *Authority of county to levy tax or license fee.* A code county shall not levy any type of tax, license fee, franchise tax, or fee which was not in effect or authorized in the code county at the time it came under the provisions of this Article, until an express authorization of the General Assembly has been enacted for this purpose by a general law which in its terms and effect applies alike to all code counties in one or more of the classes provided for in ... this Article.

Massachusetts Constitution (1780)

Declaration of Rights, Pt. I, Art. X. Each individual of the society has a right to be protected by it in the enjoyment of his life, liberty and property, according to standing laws. He is obliged, consequently, to contribute his share to the expense of this protection. . . .

Declaration of Rights, Pt. I, Art. XXIII. No subsidy, charge, tax, impost, or duties, ought to be established, fixed, laid, or levied, under any pretext whatsoever, without the consent of the people or their representatives in the legislature.

Pt. II, Ch. I, § I, Art. IV.[a] . . . full power and authority are hereby given and granted to the said general court,[b] from time to time, to make, ordain, and establish, all manner of wholesome and reasonable orders, laws, statutes, and ordinances, directions and instructions, either with penalties or without, so as the same be not repugnant or contrary to this constitution, as they shall judge to be for the good and welfare of this Commonwealth, and for the government and ordering thereof, and of the subjects of the same, and for the necessary support and defence of the government thereof; and . . . to impose and levy proportional and reasonable assessments, rates and taxes, upon all the inhabitants of, and persons resident, and estates lying, within the said Commonwealth; and also to impose and levy, reasonable duties and excises, upon any produce, goods, wares, merchandise, and commodities, whatsoever, brought into, produced, manufactured, or being within the same. . . .

And while the public charges of government, or any part thereof, shall be assessed on polls and estates, in the manner that has hitherto been practised, in order that such assessments may be made with equality, there shall be a valuation of estates within the Commonwealth taken anew once in every ten years at least, and as much oftener as the general court shall order.

Amend. Art. XLI. [Taxation of wild or forest lands.[c] **]** Full power and authority are hereby given and granted to the general court to prescribe for wild or forest lands such methods of taxation as will develop and conserve the forest resources of the commonwealth.

Amend. Art. XLIV. [Authority given to general court to tax income.] Full power and authority are hereby given and granted to the general court to impose and levy a tax on income in the manner hereinafter provided. Such tax may be at different rates upon income derived from different classes of property, but

---

[a] The text of Pt. II, Ch. I, § I, Art. IV, has been amended. See appendix B.

[b] The legislative body.

[c] The text of Amend. Art. XLI has been amended. See appendix B.

shall be levied at a uniform rate throughout the commonwealth upon incomes derived from the same class of property. The general court may tax income not derived from property at a lower rate than income derived from property, and may grant reasonable exemptions and abatements. Any class of property the income from which is taxed under the provisions of this article may be exempted from the imposition and levying of proportional and reasonable assessments, rates and taxes as at present authorized by the constitution. This article shall not be construed to limit the power of the general court to impose and levy reasonable duties and excises.

Amend. Art. XCIX. [Amendments—Valuation of agricultural and horticultural lands for purposes of taxation.] Full power and authority are hereby given and granted to the general court to prescribe, for the purpose of developing and conserving agricultural or horticultural lands, that such lands shall be valued, for the purpose of taxation, according to their agricultural or horticultural uses; provided, however, that no parcel of land which is less than five acres in area or which has not been actively devoted to agricultural or horticultural uses for the two years preceding the tax year shall be valued at less than fair market value under this article.

Michigan Constitution (1964)

Art. VII, § 16. ... The ad valorem property tax imposed for road purposes by any county shall not exceed in any year one-half of one percent of the assessed valuation for the preceding year.

Art. VII, § 21. The legislature shall provide by general laws for the incorporation of cities and villages. Such laws shall limit their rate of ad valorem property taxation for municipal purposes, and restrict the powers of cities and villages to borrow money and contract debts. Each city and village is granted power to levy other taxes for public purposes, subject to limitations and prohibitions provided by this constitution or by law.

Art. IX, § 2. The power of taxation shall never be surrendered, suspended or contracted away.

Art. IX, § 3. [**Property taxation; uniformity, assessments, classes.**] The legislature shall provide for the uniform general ad valorem taxation of real and tangible personal property not exempt by law. The legislature shall provide for the determination of true cash value of such property; the proportion of true cash value at which such property shall be uniformly assessed, which shall not, after January 1, 1966, exceed 50 percent; and for a system of equalization of assessments. The legislature may provide for alternative means of taxation of designated real and tangible personal property in lieu of general ad valorem taxation. Every tax other than the general ad valorem property tax shall be uniform upon the class or classes on which it operates.

Art. IX, § 4. [**Exemption of religious or educational nonprofit organizations.**] Property owned and occupied by non-profit religious or educational organizations and used exclusively for religious or educational purposes, as defined by law, shall be exempt from real and personal property taxes.

Art. IX, § 5. [**Assessment of property of public service businesses.**] The legislature shall provide for the assessment by the state of the property of those public service businesses assessed by the state at the date this constitution becomes effective, and of other property as designated by the legislature, and for the imposition and collection of taxes thereon. Property assessed by the state shall be assessed at the same proportion of its true cash value as the legislature shall specify for property subject to general ad valorem taxation. The rate of taxation on such property shall be the average rate levied upon other property in this state under the general ad valorem tax law, or, if the legislature provides, the rate of tax applicable to the property of each business enterprise assessed by the state shall be the average rate of ad valorem taxation levied upon other property in all counties in which any of such property is situated.

Art. IX, § 6. Except as otherwise provided in this constitution, the total amount of general ad valorem taxes imposed upon real and tangible personal property for all purposes in any one year shall not exceed 15 mills on each dollar of the assessed valuation of property as finally equalized. Under procedures provided by law, which shall guarantee the right of initiative, separate tax limitations for any county and for the townships and for school districts therein, the aggregate of which shall not exceed 18 mills on each dollar of such valuation, may be adopted and thereafter altered by the vote of a majority of the qualified electors of such county voting thereon, in lieu of the limitation hereinbefore established. These limitations may be increased to an aggregate of not to exceed 50 mills on each dollar of valuation, for a period of not to exceed 20 years at any one time, if approved by a majority of the electors, qualified under . . . this constitution, voting on the question.

The foregoing limitations shall not apply to taxes imposed for the payment of principal and interest on bonds[a] or other evidences of indebtedness[b] or for the payment of assessments or contract obligations in anticipation of which bonds are issued[c], which taxes may be imposed without limitation as to rate or amount;[d] or to taxes imposed for any other purpose by any city, village, charter county, charter township, charter authority or other authority, the tax limitations of which are provided by charter or by general law.

In any school district which extends into two or more counties, property taxes at the highest rate available in the county which contains the greatest part of the area of the district may be imposed and collected for school purposes throughout the district.

Art. IX, § 7. [**Income tax.**] No income tax graduated as to rate or base shall be imposed by the state or any of its subdivisions.

Art. IX, § 8. [**Sales tax.**] The legislature shall not impose a sales tax on retailers at a rate of more than 4% of their gross tangible personal property.

. . . .

[a,b,c] A November 1978 amendment to the constitution added the following words in each of the three places indicated: "APPROVED BY THE ELECTORS."

[d] A November 1978 amendment to the constitution inserted at this point the following words: "OR, SUBJECT TO THE PROVISIONS OF SECTIONS 25 THROUGH 34 OF THIS ARTICLE,". See Appendix B for the November 1978 Amendment containing the foregoing sections.

Minnesota Constitution
(1857. Renumbered 1974)

Art. X, § 1. The power of taxation shall never be surrendered, suspended or contracted away. Taxes shall be uniform upon the same class of subjects and shall be levied and collected for public purposes, but public burying grounds, public school houses, public hospitals, academies, colleges, universities, all seminaries of learning, all churches, church property, houses of worship, institutions of purely public charity, and public property used exclusively for any public purpose, shall be exempt from taxation except as provided in this section. . . . The legislature may authorize municipal corporations to levy and collect assessments for local improvements upon property benefited thereby without regard to cash valuation. The legislature by law may define or limit the property exempt under this section other than churches, houses of worship, and property solely used for educational purposes by academies, colleges, universities and seminaries of learning.

Art. X, § 2. To encourage and promote forestation and reforestation of lands whether owned by private persons or the public, laws may be enacted fixing in advance a definite and limited annual tax on the lands for a term of years and imposing a yield tax on the timber and other forest products at or after the end of the term.

Art. X, § 3. Every person engaged in the business of mining or producing iron ore or other ores in this state shall pay to the state an occupation tax on the valuation of all ores mined or produced, which tax shall be in addition to all other taxes provided by law. . . .

Art. XII, § 1. . . .The legislature shall pass no local or special law . . . exempting property from taxation. . . .

Art. XIV, § 9. The legislature by law may tax motor vehicles using the public streets and highways on a more onerous basis than other personal property. . . .

Mississippi Constitution (1890)

Art. IV, § 70. No revenue bill, or any bill providing for assessments of property for taxation, shall become a law except by a vote of at least three-fifths of the members of each house present and voting.

Art. IV, § 80. [**Municipal Corporations; Abuse of Power.**]
Provision shall be made by general laws to prevent the abuse by cities, towns, and other municipal corporations of their powers of assessment, taxation, borrowing money, and contracting debts.

Art. IV, § 90. The legislature shall not pass local, private, or special laws in any of the following enumerated cases, but such matters shall be provided for only by general laws, viz.:

. . . .

(h) Exemption of property from taxation or from levy or sale. . . .

Art. IV, § 112. [**Taxation and Assessment.**]
Taxation shall be uniform and equal throughout the state. Property shall be taxed in proportion to its value. Property shall be assessed for taxes under general laws, and by uniform rules, and in proportion to its value. But the legislature may provide for a special mode of valuation and assessment for railroads, and railroad and other corporate property, or for particular species of property belonging to persons, corporations, or associations not situated wholly in one county. But all such property shall be assessed in proportion to its value, and no county, or other taxing authority, shall be denied the right to levy county and special taxes upon such assessment as in other cases of property situated and assessed in the county. But the legislature may provide a special mode of assessment, fixing the taxable year, date of the tax lien, and method and date of assessing and collecting taxes on all motor vehicles.

Art. VII, § 181. [**Taxation of Corporate Property.**]
The property of all private corporations for pecuniary gain shall be taxed in the same way and to the same extent as the property of individuals, but the legislature may provide for the taxation of banks . . . by taxing the shares according to the value thereof . . . exclusive of real estate, which shall be taxed as other real estate. Exemptions from taxation to which corporations are legally entitled at the adoption of this Constitution, shall remain in full force and effect for the time of such exemption as expressed in their respective charters, or by general laws, unless sooner repealed by the legislature . . . and the legislature may impose privilege taxes on building and loan associations in lieu of all other taxes except on their real estate.

Mississippi Constitution

Art. VII, § 182. [Tax Exemptions.]

The power to tax corporations and their property shall never be surrendered or abridged by any contract or grant to which the State or any political subdivision thereof may be a party, except that the Legislature may grant exemption from taxation in the encouragement of manufactures and other enterprises of public utility extending for a period of not exceeding ten (10) years on each such enterprise hereafter constructed, and may grant exemptions not exceeding ten (10) years on each addition thereto or expansion thereof, and may grant exemptions not exceeding ten (10) years on future additions to or expansions of existing manufactures and other enterprises of public utility. The time of each exemption shall commence from the date of completion of the new enterprise, and from the date of completion of each addition or expansion, for which an exemption is granted. When the Legislature grants such exemptions for a period of ten (10) years or less, it shall be done by general laws, which shall distinctly enumerate the classes of manufactures and other law enterprises of public utility, entitled to such exemptions, and shall prescribe the mode and manner in which the right to such exemptions shall be determined.

Art. VII, § 192. [Local Tax Exemption.]

Provision shall be made by general laws whereby cities and towns may be authorized to aid and encourage the establishment of manufactories, gasworks, waterworks, and other enterprises of public utility other than railroads, within the limits of said cities or towns, by exempting all property used for such purposes from municipal taxation for a period not longer than ten years.

Art. XI, § 236. [Levee Taxes.]

The legislature shall impose for levee purposes, in addition to the levee taxes heretofore levied or authorized by law, a uniform tax of not less than two nor more than five cents an acre per annum upon every acre of land now or hereafter embraced within the limits of either or both of said levee districts . . . all reductions in such taxation shall be uniform in each of said districts; but the rate of taxation need not be the same in both of them. . . .

Art. XI, § 237. [Tax for Levee Districts.]

The legislature shall have full power to provide such system of taxation for said levee districts as it shall, from time to time, deem wise and proper.

Missouri Constitution (1945)

Art. III, § 40. The general assembly shall not pass any local or special laws:
. . . .
(8) extending the time for the assessment or collection of taxes, or otherwise relieving any assessor or collector of taxes from the due performance of their duties, or their securities from liability. . . .

Art. III, § 43. . . . No tax shall be imposed on lands the property of the United States; nor shall lands belonging to persons residing without the state ever be taxed at a higher rate than lands belonging to persons residing within the state.

Art. VI, § 18(d). The county shall only impose such taxes as it is authorized to impose by the Constitution or by law.

Art. X, § 1. Taxing power—exercise by state and local governments.—The taxing power may be exercised by the general assembly for state purposes, and by counties and other political subdivisions under power granted to them by the general assembly for county, municipal and other corporate purposes.

Art. X, § 2. Inalienability of power to tax.—The power to tax shall not be surrendered, suspended or contracted away, except as authorized by this Constitution.

Art. X, § 3. Limitation of taxation to public purposes—uniformity—general laws—time for payment of taxes—valuation.—Taxes may be levied and collected for public purposes only, and shall be uniform upon the same class of subjects within the territorial limits of the authority levying the tax. All taxes shall be levied and collected by general laws and shall be payable during the fiscal or calendar year in which the property is assessed. Except as otherwise provided in this Constitution, the methods of determining the value of property for taxation shall be fixed by law.

Art. X, § 4(a). Classification of taxable property—taxes on franchises, incomes, excises, and licenses.—All taxable property shall be classified for tax purposes as follows: Class 1, real property; Class 2, tangible personal property; Class 3, intangible personal property. The general assembly, by general law, may provide for further classification within Classes 2 and 3, based solely on the nature and characteristics of the property, and not on the nature, residence or business of the owner, or the amount owned. Nothing in this section shall prevent the taxing of franchises, privileges or incomes, or the levying of excise or motor vehicle license taxes, or any other taxes of the same or different types.

Art. X, § 4(b). Basis of assessment of tangible property—taxation of

intangibles—limitation.—Property in Classes 1 and 2 and subclasses of Class 2, shall be assessed for tax purposes as its value or such percentage of its value as may be fixed by law for each class and for each subclass of Class 2. Property in Class 3 and its subclasses shall be taxed only to the extent authorized and at the rate fixed by law for each class and subclass, and the tax shall be based on the annual yield and shall not exceed eight per cent thereof.

Art. X, § 5. Taxation of railroads.—All railroad corporations in this state, or doing business therein, shall be subject to taxation for state, county, school, municipal and other purposes, on the real and personal property owned or used by them, and on their gross earnings, their net earnings, their franchises and their capital stock.

Art. X, § 6. Property exempt from taxation.—All property, real and personal, of the state, counties and other political subdivisions, and nonprofit cemeteries, shall be exempt from taxation; and all property, real and personal, not held for private or corporate profit and used exclusively for religious worship, for schools and colleges, for purposes purely charitable, or for agricultural and horticultural societies may be exempted from taxation by general law . . . All laws exempting from taxation property other than the property enumerated in this Article, shall be void.

Art. X, § 6(a). Homestead exemption authorized.—The general assembly may provide that a portion of the valuation of real property actually occupied by the owner or owners thereof, who are over the age of sixty-five, as a homestead, be exempted from the payment of taxes thereon, in such amounts and upon such conditions as may be determined by law, or the general assembly may provide for certain tax credits or rebates in lieu of such an exemption, but any such law shall further provide for restitution to the respective political subdivisions of revenues lost by reason of the exemption, and any such law may also provide for comparable financial relief to persons of such ages who are not the owners of homesteads but who occupy rental property as their homes.

Art. X, § 6(b). The general assembly may by general law exempt from taxation all intangible property. . . .

Art. X, § 7. Relief from taxation—forest lands—obsolete, decadent, or blighted areas—limitations—exception.—For the purpose of encouraging forestry when lands are devoted exclusively to such purpose, and the reconstruction, redevelopment, and rehabilitation of obsolete, decadent, or blighted areas, the general assembly by general law may provide for such partial relief from taxation of the lands devoted to any such purpose, and of the improvements thereon, by such method or methods, for such period or periods of time, not exceeding twenty-five years in any instance, and upon such terms, conditions, and restrictions as it may prescribe; provided, however, that in the case of forest lands, the limitation of twenty-five years herein described shall not apply.

Art. X, § 8. Limitation on state tax rate on tangible property.—The state tax on real and tangible personal property, exclusive of the tax necessary to pay any bonded debt of the state, shall not exceed ten cents on the hundred dollars assessed valuation.

Art. X, § 10(a). Exclusion of state from local taxation for local purposes.—Except as provided in this Constitution, the general assembly shall not impose taxes upon counties or other political subdivisions or upon the inhabitants or property thereof for municipal, county or other corporate purposes.

Art. X, § 11(a). Taxing jurisdiction of local governments—limitation on assessed valuation.—Taxes may be levied by counties and other political subdivisions on all property subject to their taxing power, but the assessed valuation therefor in such other political subdivisions shall not exceed the assessed valuation of the same property for state and county purposes.

Art. X, § 11(b). Limitations on local tax rates.—Any tax imposed upon such property by municipalities, counties or school districts, for their respective purposes, shall not exceed the following annual rates:

For municipalities—one dollar on the hundred dollars assessed valuation;

For counties—thirty-five cents on the hundred dollars assessed valuation in counties having three hundred million dollars, or more, assessed valuation and having by operation of law attained the classification of a county of the first class; and fifty cents on the hundred dollars assessed valuation in all other counties;

For school districts formed of cities and towns, including the school district of the city of St. Louis—one dollar and twenty-five cents on the hundred dollars assessed valuation;

For all other school districts—sixty-five cents on the hundred dollars assessed valuation.

Art. X, § 11(f). Authorization of local taxes other than ad valorem taxes.—Nothing in this constitution shall prevent the enactment of any general law permitting any county or other political subdivision to levy taxes other than ad valorem taxes for its essential purposes.

Art. X, § 12(a).[a] **Additional tax rates for county roads and bridges. . .**—In addition to the rates authorized in section 11 for the county purposes, the county court in the several counties not under township organization, the

---

[a]This section has been replaced by a new art. X, § 12(a). A new art. X, § 10(c) has also been added to the constitution. See appendix B for November 1978 amendments.

township board of directors in the counties under township organization, and the proper administrative body in counties adopting an alternative form of government, may levy an additional tax, not exceeding thirty-five cents on each hundred dollars assessed valuation, all of such tax to be collected and turned in to the county treasury to be used for road and bridge purposes. . . .

Amend. 1976. Art. IV, § 43(a). Sales tax, use for conservation purposes.—For the purpose of providing additional moneys to be expended and used by the Conservation Commission, Department of Conservation, for the control, management, restoration, conservation and regulation of the bird, fish, game, forestry and wildlife resources of the state, including the purchase or other acquisition of property for said purposes, and for the administration of laws pertaining thereto, an additional sales tax . . . and an additional use tax of one-eighth of one percent is levied and imposed. . . .

Montana Constitution (1972)

Art. VIII, § 1. Tax purposes. Taxes shall be levied by general laws for public purposes.

Art. VIII, § 2. Tax power inalienable. The power to tax shall never be surrendered, suspended, or contracted away.

Art. VIII, § 3. Property tax administration. The state shall appraise, assess, and equalize the valuation of all property which is to be taxed in the manner provided by law.

Art. VIII, § 4. Equal valuation. All taxing jurisdictions shall use the assessed valuation of property established by the state.

Art. VIII, § 5. Property tax exemptions. (1) The legislature may exempt from taxation:

(a) Property of the United States, the state, counties, cities, towns, school districts, municipal corporations, and public libraries, but any private interest in such property may be taxed separately.

(b) Institutions of purely public charity, hospitals and places of burial not used or held for private or corporate profit, places for actual religious worship, and property used exclusively for educational purposes.

(c) Any other classes of property.

(2) The legislature may authorize creation of special improvement districts for capital improvements and the maintenance thereof. It may authorize the assessment of charges for such improvements and maintenance against tax exempt property directly benefited thereby.

Art. IX, § 2. . . . (2) The legislature shall provide for a fund, to be known as the resource indemnity trust of the state of Montana, to be funded by such taxes on the extraction of natural resources as the legislature may, from time to time impose for that purpose.

. . . .

ORDINANCE NO. I. FEDERAL RELATIONS . . . Second.[a] . . . the lands belonging to citizens of the United States, residing without the said state of Montana, shall never be taxed [sic] a higher rate than the lands belonging to residents thereof; . . . no taxes shall be imposed by the said state of Montana on lands or property therein belonging to, or which may hereafter be purchased by the United States or reserved for its use. . . .

---

[a] Similar to language of the Enabling Act, § 4 (Second), not repeated herein.

Nebraska Constitution
(1875. Rev. 1920)

Art. VIII, § 1.[a] The necessary revenue of the state and its governmental subdivisions shall be raised by taxation in such manner as the Legislature may direct. Taxes shall be levied by valuation uniformly and proportionately upon all tangible property and franchises, except that the Legislature may provide a different method of taxing motor vehicles.... The Legislature may enact laws to provide that the value of land actively devoted to agricultural or horticultural use shall, for property tax purposes, be that value which such land has for agricultural or horticultural use without regard to any value which such land might have for other purposes or uses, and prescribe standards and methods for the determination of the value of real or other tangible property at uniform and proportionate values. Taxes uniform as to class of property or the ownership or use thereof may be levied by valuation or otherwise upon classes of intangible property as the Legislature may determine.... Taxes other than property taxes, may be authorized by law....

Art. VIII, § 1A. [Prohibition on state property tax.] The state shall be prohibited from levying a property tax for state purposes.

Art. VIII, § 2. [Exemption of property from taxation.] The property of the state and its governmental subdivisions shall be exempt from taxation. The Legislature by general law may exempt property owned by and used exclusively for agricultural and horticultural societies, and property owned and used exclusively for educational, religious, charitable, or cemetery purposes, when such property is not owned or used for financial gain or profit to either the owner or user.... The legislature by general law may provide that the increased value of land by reason of shade or ornamental trees planted along the highway shall not be taken into account in the assessment of such land. The value of a home substantially contributed by the Veterans' Administration of the United States for a paraplegic veteran or multiple amputee shall be exempt from taxation during the life of such veteran or until the death of his widow or her remarriage.... The Legislature may classify personal property in such manner as it sees fit, and may exempt any of such classes, or may exempt all personal property from taxation. No property shall be exempt from taxation except as provided in the Constitution. The Legislature may by general law provide that a portion of the value of any residence actually occupied as a homestead by any classification of owners as determined by the Legislature shall be exempt from taxation.

Art. VIII, § 4. [Legislature has no power to remit taxes; exception.] Except as to tax and assessment charges against real property remaining delinquent and

---
[a]This section has been amended November 1978. See appendix B.

unpaid for a period of fifteen years or longer, the Legislature shall have no power to release or discharge any county, city, township, town, or district whatever, or the inhabitants thereof, or any corporation, or the property therein, from their or its proportionate share of taxes to be levied for state purposes, or due any municipal corporation, nor shall commutation for such taxes be authorized in any form whatever; Provided, that the Legislature may provide by law for the payment or cancellation of taxes or assessments against real estate remaining unpaid against real estate owned or acquired by the state or its governmental subdivisions.

Art. VIII, § 5. [County taxes, limitation.] County authorities shall never assess taxes the aggregate of which shall exceed fifty cents per one hundred dollars actual valuation as determined by the assessment rolls, except for the payment of indebtedness existing at the adoption hereof, unless authorized by a vote of the people of the county.

Art. VIII, § 6. [Local improvements of cities, towns and villages.] The Legislature may vest the corporate authorities of cities, towns and villages, with power to make local improvements, including facilities for providing off-street parking for vehicles, by special assessments or by special taxation of property benefited, and to redetermine and reallocate from time to time the benefits arising from the acquisition of such off-street parking facilities, and the Legislature may vest the corporate authorities of cities and villages with power to levy special assessments for the maintenance, repair and reconstruction of such off-street parking facilities. For all other corporate purposes, all municipal corporations may be vested with authority to assess and collect taxes, but such taxes shall be uniform in respect to persons and property within the jurisdiction of the body imposing the same, except that cities and villages may be empowered by the Legislature to assess and collect separate and additional taxes within off-street parking districts created by and within any city or village on such terms as the Legislature may prescribe.

Art. VIII, § 7. ... The Legislature shall not impose taxes upon municipal corporations, or the inhabitants or property thereof, for corporate purposes.

Art. VIII, § 10. ... the Legislature is authorized to substitute a basis other than valuation for taxes upon grain and seed produced or handled in this state. ...

Art. XIII, § 2. ... The Legislature may authorize any county, incorporated city or village, including cities operating under home rule charters, to acquire, own, develop, and lease real and personal property suitable for use by manufacturing or industrial enterprises. ... Any such real or personal property so acquired, owned, developed or used by any such county, city or village, shall be subject to taxation to the same extent as private property during the time it is leased to or held by private interests. ...

Nevada Constitution (1864)

Art. 8, § 2. Corporate property subject to taxation; exemptions. All real property, and possessory rights to the same, as well as personal property in this State, belonging to corporations now existing or hereafter created shall be subject to taxation, the same as property of individuals; Provided, that the property of corporations formed for Municipal, Charitable, Religious, or Educational purposes may be exempted by law.

Art. 8, § 8. Municipal corporations formed under general laws. The legislature shall provide for the organization of cities and towns by general laws and shall restrict their power of taxation, assessment, borrowing money, contracting debts and loaning their credit, except for procuring supplies of water; *provided, however,* that the legislature may, by general laws, in the manner and to the extent therein provided, permit and authorize the electors of any city or town to frame, adopt and amend a charter for its own government, or to amend any existing charter of such city or town.

Art. 9, § 2. The legislature shall provide by law for an annual tax sufficient to defray the estimated expenses of the state for each fiscal year. . . .

Art. 10, § 1. The legislature shall provide by law for a uniform and equal rate of assessment and taxation, and shall prescribe such regulations as shall secure a just valuation for taxation of all property, real, personal and possessory, except mines and mining claims, when not patented, the proceeds alone of which shall be assessed and taxed, and when patented, each patented mine shall be assessed at not less than five hundred dollars ($500), except when one hundred dollars ($100) in labor has been actually performed on such patented mine during the year, in addition to the tax upon the net proceeds . . . mortgages . . . are deemed to represent interest in property already assessed and taxed, either in Nevada or elsewhere, and shall be exempt. Notwithstanding the provisions of this section, the legislature may constitute agricultural and open-space real property having a greater value for another use than that for which it is being used, as a separate class for taxation purposes and may provide a separate uniform plan for appraisal and valuation of such property for assessment purposes. If such plan is provided, the legislature shall also provide for retroactive assessment for a period of not less than 7 years when agricultural and open-space real property is converted to a higher use conforming to the use for which other nearby property is used. . . . No inheritance or estate tax shall ever be levied, and there shall also be excepted such property as may be exempted by law for municipal, educational, literary, scientific or other charitable purposes.[a]

Art. 10, § 2. Total tax levy for public purposes limited. The total tax levy for all public purposes including levies for bonds, within the state, or any subdivision thereof, shall not exceed five cents on one dollar of assessed valuation.

ORDINANCE ... Third. ... lands belonging to citizens of the United States, residing without the said state, shall never be taxed higher than the land belonging to the residents thereof; and ... no taxes shall be imposed by said state on lands or property therein belonging to, or which may hereafter be purchased by, the United States, unless otherwise provided by the congress of the United States.

---

[a] A November 1978 amendment added prior to the last sentence a provision phasing out the business inventory tax, and added: "The legislature may exempt any other personal property, including livestock."

New Hampshire Constitution (1784)

Pt. I, [Art.] 12th. Every member of the community has a right to be protected by it, in the enjoyment of his life, liberty, and property; he is therefore bound to contribute his share in the expense of such protection, and to yield his personal service when necessary. . . .

Pt. I, [Art.] 28th. No subsidy, charge, tax, impost, or duty, shall be established, fixed, laid, or levied, under any pretext whatsoever, without the consent of the people, or their representatives in the legislature, or authority derived from that body.

Pt. II, [Art.] 5th. . . . full power and authority are hereby given and granted to the . . . general court[a] . . . to impose and levy proportional and reasonable assessments, rates, and taxes, upon all the inhabitants of, and residents within, the said state; and upon all estates within the same. . . . For the purpose of encouraging conservation of the forest resources of the state, the general court may provide for special assessments, rates and taxes on growing wood and timber.

Pt. II, [Art.] 5B. The general court may provide for the assessment of any class of real estate at valuations based upon the current use thereof.

Pt. II, [Art.] 6th. The public charges of government, or any part thereof, may be raised by taxation, upon polls, estates, and other classes of property, including franchises and property when passing by will or inheritance; and there shall be a valuation of the estates within the state taken anew once in every five years, at least, and as much oftener as the general court shall order.

---

[a]The legislative body.

New Jersey Constitution (1947)

Art. VIII, § 1, para. 1. Taxation; assessment.

(a) Property shall be assessed for taxation under general laws and by uniform rules. All real property assessed and taxed locally or by the State for allotment and payment to taxing districts shall be assessed according to the same standard of value, except as otherwise permitted herein, and such real property shall be taxed at the general tax rate of the taxing district in which the property is situated, for the use of such taxing district.

(b) The Legislature shall enact laws to provide that the value of land, not less than 5 acres in area, which is determined by the assessing officer of the taxing jurisdiction to be actively devoted to agricultural or horticultural use and to have been so devoted for at least the 2 successive years immediately preceding the tax year in issue, shall, for local tax purposes, on application of the owner, be that value which such land has for agricultural or horticultural use.

Any such laws shall provide that when land which has been valued in this manner for local tax purposes is applied to a use other than for agriculture or horticulture it shall be subject to additional taxes in an amount equal to the difference, if any, between the taxes paid or payable on the basis of the valuation and the assessment authorized hereunder and the taxes that would have been paid or payable had the land been valued and assessed as otherwise provided in this Constitution, in the current year and in such of the tax years immediately preceding, not in excess of 2 such years in which the land was valued as herein authorized.

Such laws shall also provide for the equilization of assessments of land valued in accordance with the provisions hereof and for the assessment and collection of any additional taxes levied thereupon and shall include such other provisions as shall be necessary to carry out the provisions of this amendment.

Art. VIII, § 1, para. 2. Taxation; exemptions, in general.

Exemption from taxation may be granted only by general laws. Until otherwise provided by law all exemptions from taxation validly granted and now in existence shall be continued. Exemptions from taxation may be altered or repealed, except those exempting real and personal property used exclusively for religious, educational, charitable or cemetery purposes, as defined by law, and owned by any corporation or association organized and conducted exclusively for one or more of such purposes and not operating for profit.

Art. VIII, § 1, para. 3. Taxation; exemptions, veterans and widows of veterans.

Any citizen and resident of this State now or hereafter honorably discharged or released under honorable circumstances from active service, in time of war or of other emergency as, from time to time, defined by the Legislature, in any branch of the Armed Forces of the United States shall be entitled, annually, to a deduction from the amount of any tax bill for taxes on real and personal property, or both, in the sum of $50.00, or if the amount of any such tax bill shall be less than $50.00, to a cancellation thereof, which deduction or cancellation shall not be altered or repealed. . . . Any person . . . who has . . . a service-connected disability, shall be entitled to such further deduction from taxation as from time to time may be provided by law. The widow . . . shall be entitled, during her widowhood . . . to the deduction or cancellation. . . .

Art. VIII, § 1, para. 4. The Legislature may, from time to time, enact laws granting an annual deduction from the amount of any tax bill for taxes on the real property of any citizen and resident of this State of the age of 65 or more years, or any citizen and resident of this State less than 65 years of age who is permanently and totally disabled according to the provisions of the Federal Social Security Act, residing in a dwelling house owned by him which is a constituent part of such real property but no such deduction shall be in excess of $160.00 and such deduction shall be restricted to owners having an income not in excess of $5,000.00 per year exclusive of [various retirement] benefits. . . .
. . . .

The surviving spouse of a deceased citizen and resident of this State who during his or her life received a real property tax deduction pursuant to this paragraph shall be entitled, so long as he or she shall remain unmarried and a resident in the same dwelling house with respect to which said deduction was granted, to the same deduction, upon the same conditions, with respect to the same real property, notwithstanding that said surviving spouse is under the age of 65 and is not permanently and totally disabled, provided that said surviving spouse is 55 years of age or older.

Any such deduction when so granted by law shall be granted so that it will not be in addition to any other deduction or exemption to which the said citizen and resident may be entitled, but said citizen and resident may receive in addition any homestead rebate or credit provided by law. . . .

Art. VIII, § 1, para. 5. The Legislature may adopt a homestead statute which entitles homeowners, residential tenants and net lease residential tenants to a rebate or a credit of a sum of money related to property taxes paid by or allocable to them at such rates, and subject to such limits, as may be provided by law. Such rebates or credits may include a differential rebate or credit to citizens and residents who are of the age of 65 or more years, or less than 65 years of age who are permanently and totally disabled . . . or are 55 years of age or more and the surviving spouse. . . .

Art. VIII, § 1, para. 6. The Legislature may enact general laws under which municipalities may adopt ordinances granting exemptions or abatements from taxation on buildings and structures in areas declared in need of rehabilitation in accordance with statutory criteria, within such municipalities and to the land comprising the premises upon which such buildings or structures are erected and which is necessary for a fair enjoyment thereof. Such exemptions shall be for limited periods of time as specified by law, but not in excess of 5 years.

Art. VIII, § 1, para. 7. No tax shall be levied on personal incomes of individuals, estates and trusts of this State unless the entire net receipts therefrom shall be received into the treasury, placed in a perpetual fund and be annually appropriated, pursuant to formulas established from time to time by the Legislature, to the several counties, municipalities and school districts of this State exclusively for the purpose of reducing or offsetting property taxes.

New Mexico Constitution (1912)

Art. IV, § 24. The legislature shall not pass local or special laws in any of the following cases . . . the assessment or collection of taxes or extending the time of collection thereof . . . remitting fines, penalties, forfeitures or taxes . . . exempting property from taxation. . . .

Art. VIII, § 1. [Taxation; ad valorem; equality; limitation on percentage of value.]

Taxes levied upon tangible property shall be in proportion to the value thereof, and taxes shall be equal and uniform upon subjects of taxation of the same class. Different methods may be provided by law to determine value of different kinds of property, but the percentage of value against which tax rates are assessed shall not exceed thirty-three and one-third percent.

Art. VIII, § 2. [Property tax limits; exceptions.]

Taxes levied upon real or personal property for state revenue shall not exceed four mills annually on each dollar of the assessed valuation thereof except for the support of the educational, penal and charitable institutions of the state, payment of the state debt and interest thereon; and the total annual tax levy upon such property for all state purposes exclusive of necessary levies for the state debt shall not exceed ten mills; Provided, however, that taxes levied upon real or personal tangible property for all purposes, except special levies on specific classes of property and except necessary levies for public debt, shall not exceed twenty mills annually on each dollar of the assessed valuation thereof, but laws may be passed authorizing additional taxes to be levied outside of such limitation when approved by at least a majority of the qualified electors of the taxing district who paid a property tax therein during the preceding year voting on such proposition.

Art. VIII, § 3. [Tax exempt property.]

The property of the United States, the state and all counties, towns, cities and school districts, and other municipal corporations, public libraries, community ditches and all laterals thereof, all church property not used for commercial purposes, all property used for educational or charitable purposes, all cemeteries not used or held for private or corporate profit . . . shall be exempt from taxation. . . .

Art. VIII, § 5. [Exemptions for heads of families and veterans.]

The Legislature may exempt from taxation property of each head of the family to the amount of two hundred dollars ($200) and the property, including the community or joint property of husband and wife, of every honorably discharged member of the armed forces of the United States who served in such armed forces during any period in which they were or are engaged in armed conflict . . . and the widow or widower of every such . . . member . . . in the sum of two thousands dollars ($2,000). . . .

Art. VIII, § 6. [Assessment of lands.]
Lands held in large tracts shall not be assessed for taxation at any lower value per acre then [than] lands of the same character or quality and similarly situated, held in smaller tracts. The plowing of land shall not be considered as adding value thereto for the purpose of taxation.

Art. VIII, § 9. [Exception to local taxing power.]
No tax or assessment of any kind shall be levied by any political subdivision whose enabling legislation does not provide for an elected governing authority. This section does not prohibit the levying or collection of a tax or special assessment by an initial appointed governing authority where the appointed governing authority will be replaced by an elected one within six years of the date the appointed authority takes office. . . .

Art. X, § 4. (a) The legislature shall, by general law, provide for the formation of combined city and county municipal corporations, and for the manner of determining the territorial limits thereof, each of which shall be known as a "city and county," and, when organized, shall contain a population of at least fifty thousand (50,000) inhabitants. . . .

Art. X, § 4. (c) No city or county government existing outside the territorial limits of such city and county shall exercise any police, taxation or other powers within the territorial limits of such city and county, but all such powers shall be exercised by the city and county and the officers thereof, subject to such constitutional provisions and general laws as apply to either cities or counties.
. . . .

Art. XXI, §2. . . . the lands and other property belonging to citizens of the United States residing without this state shall never be taxed at a higher rate than the lands and other property belonging to residents thereof . . . no taxes shall be imposed by this state upon lands or property therein belonging to or which may hereafter be acquired by the United States or reserved for its use; but nothing herein shall preclude this state from taxing as other lands and property are taxed, any lands and other property outside of an Indian reservation, owned or held by any Indian, save and except such lands as have been granted or acquired as aforesaid, or as may be granted or confirmed to any Indian or Indians under any Act of Congress; but all such lands shall be exempt from taxation by this state so long and to such extent as the Congress of the United States has prescribed or may hereafter prescribe.

Amend. Art. VIII. [Unnumbered Section]. There shall be deposited in a permanent trust fund known as the "severance tax permanent fund" that part of state revenue derived from excise taxes which have been, or shall be, designated severance taxes imposed upon the severance of natural resources within this state. . . .

New York Constitution (1895. Rev. 1938)

Art. III, § 17. The legislature shall not pass a private or local bill in any of the following cases:

. . . .

Granting to any person, association, firm or corporation, an exemption from taxation on real or personal property.

. . . .

Art. VIII, § 10. Hereafter, in any county, city, village or school district described in this section, the amount to be raised by tax on real estate in any fiscal year, in addition to providing for the interest on and the principal of all indebtedness, shall not exceed an amount equal to the following percentages of the average full valuation of taxable real estate of such county, city, village or school district, less the amount to be raised by tax on real estate in such year for the payment of the interest on and redemption of certificates or other evidence of indebtedness described in . . . this article, or renewals thereof:

(a) any county, for county purposes, one and one-half per centum; provided, however, that the legislature may prescribe a method by which such limitation may be increased to not to exceed two per centum;

(b) any city of one hundred twenty-five thousand or more inhabitants according to the latest federal census, for city purposes, two per centum;

(c) any city having less than one hundred twenty-five thousand inhabitants according to the latest federal census, for city purposes, two per centum;

(d) any village, for village purposes, two per centum;

(e) any school district which is coterminous with or partly within or wholly within, a city having less than one hundred twenty-five thousand inhabitants according to the latest federal census, for school district purposes, one and one-quarter per centum . . . [exceptions raising up to two percentum; 60% voting approval]

(f) Notwithstanding the provisions of sub-paragraphs (a) and (b) of this section, the city of New York and the counties therein, for city and county purposes, a combined total of two and one-half per centum. . . .

Art. VIII, § 12. It shall be the duty of the legislature, subject to the provisions of this constitution, to restrict the power of taxation, assessment . . . of counties, cities, towns and villages, so as to prevent abuses in taxation and assessments . . . by them. Nothing in this article shall be construed to prevent the legislature from further restricting the powers herein specified of any county, city, town, village or school district . . . to levy taxes on real estate. The legislature shall not, however, restrict the power to levy taxes on real estate for the payment of interest on or principal of indebtedness theretofore contracted.

Art. IX, § 2. (c) (ii) every local government shall have power to adopt and amend local laws not inconsistent with the provisions of this constitution or any general law relating to the following subjects, whether or not they relate to the property, affairs or government of such local government, except to the extent that the legislature shall restrict the adoption of such a local law relating to other than the property, affairs or government of such local government:

. . . .

(8) The levy, collection and administration of local taxes authorized by the legislature and of assessments for local improvements, consistent with laws enacted by the legislature.

. . . .

Art. XVI, § 1. The power of taxation shall never be surrendered, suspended or contracted away, except as to securities issued for public purposes pursuant to law. Any laws which delegate the taxing power shall specify the types of taxes which may be imposed thereunder and provide for their review.

Exemptions from taxation may be granted only by general laws. Exemptions may be altered or repealed except those exempting real or personal property used exclusively for religious, educational or charitable purposes as defined by law and owned by any corporation or association organized or conducted exclusively for one or more of such purposes and not operating for profit.

Art. XVI, § 2. The legislature shall provide for the supervision, review and equalization of assessments for purposes of taxation. Assessments shall in no case exceed full value.

Nothing in this constitution shall be deemed to prevent the legislature from providing for the assessment, levy and collection of village taxes by the taxing authorities of those subdivisions of the state in which the lands comprising the respective villages are located. . . .

Art. XVI, § 3. . . . Intangible personal property shall not be taxed ad valorem nor shall any excise tax be levied solely because of the ownership or possession thereof, except that the income therefrom may be taken into consideration in computing any excise tax measured by income generally. Undistributed profits shall not be taxed.

Art. XVI, § 4. Where the state has power to tax corporations incorporated under the laws of the United States there shall be no discrimination in the rates and method of taxation between such corporations and other corporations exercising substantially similar functions and engaged in substantially similar business within the state.

Art. XVIII. [Housing and nursing home accommodations for persons of low income; slum clearance.]

§ 2. . . . the legislature may . . . grant or authorize tax exemptions in whole or in part, except that no such exemption may be granted or authorized for a period of more than sixty years. . . .

North Carolina Constitution (1971)

Art. I, § 8. Representation and taxation. The people of this State shall not be taxed or made subject to the payment of any impost or duty without the consent of themselves or their representatives in the General Assembly, freely given.

Art. II, § 24. . . . The General Assembly shall not enact any local, private, or special act or resolution:

. . . .
   (k) Extending the time for the levy or collection of taxes. . . .

Art. V, § 2. State and local taxation.
   (1) **Power of taxation.** The power of taxation shall be exercised in a just and equitable manner, for public purposes only, and shall never be surrendered, suspended, or contracted away.
   (2) **Classification.** Only the General Assembly shall have the power to classify property for taxation, which power shall be exercised only on a State-wide basis and shall not be delegated. No class of property shall be taxed except by uniform rule, and every classification shall be made by general law uniformly applicable in every county, city and town, and other unit of local government.
   (3) **Exemptions.** Property belonging to the State, counties, and municipal corporations shall be exempt from taxation. The General Assembly may exempt cemeteries and property held for educational, scientific, literary, cultural, charitable, or religious purposes, and, to a value not exceeding $300, any personal property. The General Assembly may exempt from taxation not exceeding $1,000 in value of property held and used as the place of residence of the owner. Every exemption shall be on a State-wide basis and shall be made by general law uniformly applicable in every county, city and town, and other unit of local government. No taxing authority other than the General Assembly may grant exemptions, and the General Assembly shall not delegate the powers accorded to it by this subsection.
   (4) **Special tax areas.** . . . the General Assembly may enact general laws authorizing the governing body of any county, city, or town to define territorial areas and to levy taxes within those areas, in addition to those levied throughout the county, city, or town, in order to finance, provide, or maintain services, facilities, and functions in addition to or to a greater extent than those financed, provided, or maintained for the entire county, city, or town.
   (5) **Purposes of property tax.** The General Assembly shall not authorize any county, city or town, special district, or other unit of local government to levy taxes on property, except for purposes authorized by general law uniformly applicable throughout the State, unless the tax is approved by a majority of the qualified voters of the unit who vote thereon.

(6) **Income tax.** The rate of tax on incomes shall not in any case exceed ten per cent, and there shall be allowed personal exemptions and deductions so that only net incomes are taxed.

. . . .

Art. V, § 3. ... General laws may be enacted for classes defined by population or other criteria. General laws uniformly applicable throughout the State shall be made applicable without classification or exception in every city and town, but need not be made applicable in every unit of local government in the State. General laws uniformly applicable in every county, city and town, and other unit of local government, or in every local court district, shall be made applicable without classification or exception in every unit of local government, or in every local court district, as the case may be. The General Assembly may at any time repeal any special, local, or private act.

Art. V, § 5. Acts levying taxes to state objects. Every act of the General Assembly levying a tax shall state the special object to which it is to be applied, and it shall be applied to no other purpose.

Art. V, § 9. Notwithstanding any other provision of this Constitution, the General Assembly may enact general laws to authorize counties to create authorities to issue revenue bonds to finance, but not to refinance, the cost of capital projects consisting of industrial, manufacturing and pollution control facilities for industry and pollution control facilities for public utilities. ...

... All such capital projects and all transactions therefor shall be subject to taxation to the extent such projects and transactions would be subject to taxation if no public body were involved therewith; provided, however, that the General Assembly may provide that the interest on such revenue bonds shall be exempt from income taxes within the State.

. . . .

North Dakota Constitution (1889)

Art. II, § 69. The legislative assembly shall not pass local or special laws in any of the following enumerated cases, that is to say:

. . . .

20. Granting to any corporation, association or individual . . . any special or exclusive privilege, immunity or franchise whatever.

. . . .

23. For the assessment or collection of taxes.

. . . .

25. Extending the time for the collection of taxes.

. . . .

29. Exempting property from taxation.

. . . .

Art. VI, § 130. Except in the case of home rule cities and villages as provided in this section the legislative assembly shall provide by general law for the organization of municipal corporations, restricting their powers as to levying taxes and assessments, borrowing money, and contracting debts. Money raised by taxation, loan or assessment for any purpose shall not be diverted to any other purpose except by authority of law.

. . . .

Art. XI, § 174. Taxation. The legislative assembly shall provide for raising revenue sufficient to defray the expenses of the state for each year, not to exceed in any one year four (4) mills on the dollar of the assessed valuation of all taxable property in the state, to be ascertained by the last assessment made for state and county purposes, and also a sufficient sum to pay the interest on the state debt.

Art. XI, § 175. Tax laws. No tax shall be levied except in pursuance of law, and every law imposing a tax shall state distinctly the object of the same, to which only it shall be applied. . . .

Art. XI, § 176. Uniformity of taxation; exemptions. Taxes shall be uniform upon the same class of property including franchises within the territorial limits of the authority levying the tax. The legislature may by law exempt any or all classes of personal property from taxation and within the meaning of this section, fixtures, buildings and improvements of every character, whatsoever, upon land shall be deemed personal property. The property of the United States and of the state, county and municipal corporations and property used exclusively for schools, religious, cemetery, charitable or other public purposes shall be exempt from taxation. Except as restricted by this Article, the legislature may provide for raising revenue and fixing the situs of all property for the purpose of taxation. Provided that all taxes and exemptions in force when this amendment is adopted shall remain in force until otherwise provided by statute.

Art. XI, § 177. Acreage tax. The legislature may by law provide for the levy and collection of an acreage tax on lands within the state in addition to the limitations specified in Section 174 in Article XI of the constitution. The proceeds of such tax shall be used to indemnify the owners of growing crops against damages by hail, provided that lands used exclusively for public roads, rights of way of common carriers, mining, manufacturing or pasturage may be exempt from such tax.

Art. XI, § 178. Power of taxation. The power of taxation shall never be surrendered or suspended by any grant or contract to which the state or any county or other municipal corporation shall be a party.

Art. XI, § 179. Assessment of taxable property; utilities. All taxable property except as hereinafter in this section provided, shall be assessed in the county, city, township, village or district in which it is situated, in the manner prescribed by law. The property, including franchises of all railroads operated in this state, and of all express companies, freight line companies, dining car companies, sleeping car companies, car equipment companies, or private car line companies, telegraph or telephone companies, the property of any person, firm or corporation used for the purpose of furnishing electric light, heat or power, or in distributing the same for public use, and the property of any other corporation, firm or individual now or hereafter operating in this state, and used directly or indirectly in the carrying of persons, property or messages, shall be assessed by the State Board of Equalization in a manner prescribed by such state board or commission as may be provided by law. But should any railroad allow any portion of its railway to be used for any purpose other than the operation of a railroad thereon, such portion of its railway, while so used shall be assessed in a manner provided for the assessment of other real property.

Art. XVI. COMPACT WITH THE UNITED STATES
§ 203. ... Second ... the lands belonging to citizens of the United States residing without this state shall never be taxed at a higher rate than the lands belonging to residents of this state; ... no taxes shall be imposed by this state on lands or property therein, belonging to, or which may hereafter be purchased by the United States or reserved for its use. ...

Ohio Constitution
(1851. Rev. 1912)

Art. II, § 1e. [Powers; limitations of use.]
The powers defined herein as the "initiative" and "referendum" shall not be used to pass a law authorizing any classification of property for the purpose of levying different rates of taxation thereon or of authorizing the levy of any single tax on land or land values or land sites at a higher rate or by a different rule than is or may be applied to improvements thereon or to personal property.

Art. II, § 36. [Conservation.]
Laws may be passed to encourage forestry and agriculture, and to that end areas devoted exclusively to forestry may be exempted, in whole or in part, from taxation. Notwithstanding the provisions of section 2 of Article XII, laws may be passed to provide that land devoted exclusively to agricultural use be valued for real property tax purposes at the current value such land has for such agricultural use. Laws may also be passed to provide for the deferral or recoupment of any part of the difference in the dollar amount of real property tax levied in any year on land valued in accordance with its agricultural use and the dollar amount of real property tax which would have been levied upon such land had it been valued for such year in accordance with section 2 of Article XII. . . .

Art. XII, § 2. No property, taxed according to value, shall be so taxed in excess of one per cent of its true value in money for all state and local purposes, but laws may be passed authorizing additional taxes to be levied outside of such limitation, either when approved by at least a majority of the electors of the taxing district voting on such proposition, or when provided for by the charter of a municipal corporation. Land and improvements thereon shall be taxed by uniform rule according to value, except that laws may be passed to reduce taxes by providing for a reduction in value of the homestead of permanently and totally disabled residents and residents sixty-five years of age and older, and providing for income and other qualifications to obtain such reduction. . . .

Art. XII, § 3. Laws may be passed providing for:
(A) The taxation of decedents' estates or of the right to receive or succeed to such estates, and the rates of such taxation may be uniform or may be graduated based on the value of the estate, inheritance, or succession. Such tax may also be levied at different rates upon collateral and direct inheritances, and a portion of each estate may be exempt from such taxation as provided by law.
(B) The taxation of incomes, and the rates of such taxation may be either uniform or graduated, and may be applied to such incomes and with such exemptions as may be provided by law.

(C) Excise and franchise taxes and for the imposition of taxes upon the production of coal, oil, gas, and other minerals. . . .

Art. XIII, § 4. [Corporate property subject to taxation.]

The property of corporations, now existing or hereafter created, shall forever be subject to taxation, the same as the property of individuals.

Art. XVIII, § 11. [Assessment of property to pay for local improvements.]

Any municipality appropriating private property for a public improvement may provide money therefor in part by assessments upon benefited property not in excess of the special benefits conferred upon such property by the improvements. Said assessments, however, upon all the abutting, adjacent, and other property in the district benefited, shall in no case be levied for more than fifty per centum of the cost of such appropriation.

Art. XVIII, § 13. Laws may be passed to limit the power of municipalities to levy taxes. . . .

Oklahoma Constitution (1907)

Art. I, § 3. .... Land belonging to citizens of the United States residing without the limits of the State shall never be taxed at a higher rate than the land belonging to residents thereof. No taxes shall be imposed by the State on lands or property belonging to or which may hereafter be purchased by the United States or reserved for its use.

Art. V, § 46. The Legislature shall not, except as otherwise provided in this Constitution, pass any local or special law authorizing:

....
Exempting property from taxation;
....
Extending the time for the assessment or collection of taxes. ....

Art. V, § 50. Exemption of property from taxation. — The Legislature shall pass no law exempting any property withis [within] this State from taxation, except as otherwise provided in this Constitution.

Art. X, § 5. Surrender of power of taxation—Uniformity of taxes. — The power of taxation shall never be surrendered, suspended, or contracted away. Taxes shall be uniform upon the same class of subjects.

Art. X, § 6. All property used for free public libraries, free museums, public cemeteries, property used exclusively for schools, colleges, and all property used exclusively for religious and charitable purposes, and all property of the United States, and of this State, and of counties and of municipalities of this State ... and all growing crops shall be exempt from taxation: Provided, That all property not herein specified now exempt from taxation under the laws of the Territory of Oklahoma, shall be exempt from taxation until otherwise provided by law. ...

... free homes or schools for orphan children, and for poor and indigent persons, and all ... orphan homes ... shall be exempt from taxation, and such property as may be exempt by reason of treaty stipulations, existing between the Indians and the United States government, or by Federal laws, during the force and effect of such treaties or Federal laws. The Legislature may authorize any incorporated city or town, by a majority vote of its electors voting thereon, to exempt manufacturing establishments and public utilities from municipal taxation, for a period not exceeding five years, as an inducement to their location.

Art. X, § 6A. Intangible personal property as below defined shall not be subject to ad valorem tax or to any other tax in lieu of ad valorem tax within this State:

(d) . . . except notes, debentures, and other evidences of debt secured by real estate mortgages which are subject to the Mortgage Registration Tax. . . .

. . . .

Art. X, § 7. Assessments for local improvements. — The Legislature may authorize county and municipal corporations to levy and collect assessments for local improvements upon property benefited thereby, homesteads included, without regard to a cash valuation.

Art. X, § 8. Valuation of property for taxation. — All property which may be taxed ad valorem shall be assessed for taxation at its fair cash value, estimated at the price it would bring at a fair voluntary sale, except real property and tangible personal property shall not be assessed for taxation at more than thirty-five percent (35%) of its fair cash value, estimated at the price it would bring at a fair voluntary sale. Provided, however, that no real property shall be assessed for ad valorem taxation at a value greater than thirty-five percent (35%) of its fair cash value for the highest and best use for which such property was actually used, or was previously classified for use, during the calendar year next preceding the first day of January on which the assessment is made. Provided, further, that the transfer of property without a change in its use classification shall not require a reassessment based exclusively upon the sale value of such property. In connection with the foregoing, the Legislature shall be empowered to enact laws defining classifications of use for the purpose of applying standards to facilitate uniform assessment procedures in this state. . . .

Art. X, § 9. Amount of ad valorem tax. — (a) Except as herein otherwise provided, the total taxes for all purposes on an ad valorem basis shall not exceed, in any taxable year, fifteen (15) mills on the dollar, no less than five (5) mills of which is hereby apportioned for school district purposes, the remainder to be apportioned between county, city, town and school district, by the County Excise Board, until such time as a regular apportionment thereof is otherwise provided for by the Legislature.

No ad valorem tax shall be levied for State purposes, nor shall any part of the proceeds of any ad valorem tax levy upon any kind of property in this State be used for State purposes.

. . . .

Art. X, § 12. The Legislature shall have power to provide for the levy and collection of license, franchise, gross revenue, excise, income, collateral and direct inheritance, legacy and succession taxes; also graduated income taxes, graduated collateral and direct inheritance taxes, graduated legacy and succession taxes; also stamp, registration, production or other specific taxes.

. . . .

Art. X, § 13. Independence of state taxation. — The State may select its subjects of taxation, and levy and collect its revenues independent of the counties, cities, or other municipal subdivisions.

Art. X, § 14. Taxes shall be levied and collected by general laws, and for public purposes only. . . .

Art. X, § 19. Specification of purpose of tax—Devotion to another purpose.— Every act enacted by the Legislature, and every ordinance and resolution passed by any county, city, town, or municipal board or local legislative body, levying a tax shall specify distinctly the purpose for which said tax is levied, and no tax levied and collected for one purpose shall ever be devoted to another purpose.

Art. X, § 20. Taxes for county, city, town or municipal purposes.— The Legislature shall not impose taxes for the purpose of any county, city, town, or other municipal corporation, but may, by general laws, confer on the proper authorities thereof, respectively, the power to assess and collect such taxes.

Art. X, § 22. Classification of property. — Nothing in this Constitution shall be held, or construed, to prevent the classification of property for purposes of taxation; and the valuation of different classes by different means or methods.

Art. XII-A, § 1. Exemption from ad valorem taxation authorized. — All homesteads as is or may be defined under the Laws of the State of Oklahoma for tax exemption purposes, may hereafter be exempted from all forms of ad valorem taxation by the Legislature. . . .

Art. XII-A, § 2. Duration of exemption—Increase of homestead. — Any act of the Legislature, which is authorized by this amendment and which provides that homesteads shall be exempted from ad valorem taxation, shall be in full force and effect for a period of not less than twenty years from the date of the taking effect of such act and for such time thereafter as the same shall remain without repeal or amendment by the Legislature, provided, that the homestead as defined in any such act of exemption may be increased at any time but not diminished.

Oregon Constitution (1859)

Art. I, § 32. Taxes and duties; uniformity of taxation. No tax or duty shall be imposed without the consent of the people or their representatives in the Legislative Assembly; and all taxation shall be uniform on the same class of subjects within the territorial limits of the authority levying the tax.

Art. IV, § 23. The Legislative Assembly shall not pass special or local laws, in any of the following enumerated cases, that is to say:—

. . . .

For the assessment and collection of Taxes, for State, County, Township, or road purposes. . . .

. . . .

Art. IX, § 1. Assessment and taxation; uniform rules; uniformity of operation of laws. The Legislative Assembly shall, and the people through the initiative may, provide by law uniform rules of assessment and taxation. All taxes shall be levied and collected under general laws operating uniformly throughout the State.

Art. IX, § 3. No tax shall be levied except in pursuance of law, and every law imposing a tax shall state distinctly the object of the same to which only it shall be applied. . . .

Art. XI, § 11. Tax limitation. (1) Except as provided in subsection (3) of this section, no taxing unit, whether it be the state, any county, municipality, district or other body to which the power to levy a tax has been delegated, shall in any year so exercise that power to raise a greater amount of revenue than its tax base as defined in subsection (2) of this section. The portion of any tax levied in excess of any limitation imposed by this section shall be void.

(2) The tax base of each taxing unit in a given year shall be one of the following:

(a) The amount obtained by adding six percent to the total amount of tax lawfully levied by the taxing unit, exclusive of amount described in paragraphs (a) and (b) of subsection (3) of this section, in any one of the last three years in which such a tax was levied by the unit; or

(b) An amount approved as a new tax base by a majority of the legal voters of the taxing unit voting on the question submitted to them in a form specifying in dollars and cents the amount of the tax base in effect and the amount of the tax base submitted for approval. The new tax base, if approved, shall first apply to the levy for the fiscal year next following its approval.

(3) The limitation provided in subsection (1) of this section shall not apply to:

(a) That portion of any tax levied which is for the payment of bonded indebtedness or interest thereon.

(b) That portion of any tax levied which is specifically voted outside the limitation imposed by subsection (1) of this section by a majority of the legal voters of the taxing unit voting on the question.

(4) Notwithstanding the provisions of subsections (1) to (3) of this section, the following special rules shall apply during the periods indicated:

(a) During the fiscal year following the creation of a new taxing unit which includes property previously included in a similar taxing unit, the new taxing unit and the old taxing unit may not levy amounts on the portions of property received or retained greater than the amount obtained by adding six percent to the total amount of tax lawfully levied by the old taxing unit on the portion received or retained, exclusive of amounts described in paragraphs (a) and (b) of subsection (3) of this section, in any one of the last three years in which such a tax was levied.

(b) During the fiscal year following the annexation of additional property to an existing taxing unit, the tax base of the annexing unit established under subsection (2) of this section shall be increased by an amount equal to the equalized assessed valuation of the taxable property in the annexed territory for the fiscal year of annexation multiplied by the millage rate within the tax base of the annexing unit for the fiscal year of annexation, plus six percent of such amount.

(5) The Legislative Assembly may provide for the time and manner of calling and holding elections authorized under this section. However, the question of establishing a new tax base by a taxing unit other than the state shall be submitted at a regular statewide general or primary election.

Pennsylvania Constitution (1968)

Art. III, § 31. The General Assembly shall not delegate to any special commission, private corporation or association, any power . . . to levy taxes. . . .

Art. III, § 32. The General Assembly shall pass no local or special law in any case which has been or can be provided for by general law and specifically the General Assembly shall not pass any local or special law:

. . . .

(6) Exempting property from taxation. . . .

Art. VIII, § 1. All taxes shall be uniform, upon the same class of subjects, within the territorial limits of the authority levying the tax, and shall be levied and collected under general laws.

Art. VIII, § 2. (a) The General Assembly may by law exempt from taxation:

(i) Actual places of regularly stated religious worship;

(ii) Actual places of burial, when used or held by a person or organization deriving no private or corporate profit therefrom and no substantial part of whose activity consists of selling personal property in connection therewith;

(iii) That portion of public property which is actually and regularly used for public purposes;

(iv) That portion of the property owned and occupied by any branch, post or camp of honorably discharged servicemen or servicewomen which is actually and regularly used for benevolent, charitable or patriotic purposes; and

(v) Institutions of purely public charity, but in the case of any real property tax exemptions only that portion of real property of such institution which is actually and regularly used for the purposes of the institution.

(b) The General Assembly may, by law:

(i) Establish standards and qualifications for private forest reserves, and make special provision for the taxation thereof;

(ii) Establish as a class or classes of subjects of taxation the property or privileges of persons who, because of age, disability, infirmity or poverty are determined to be in need of tax exemption or of special tax provisions, and for any such class or classes, uniform standards and qualifications. The Commonwealth, or any other taxing authority, may adopt or employ such class or classes and standards and qualifications, and except as herein provided may impose taxes, grant exemptions, or make special tax provisions in accordance therewith. No exemption or special provision shall be made under this clause with respect to taxes upon the sale or use of personal property, and no exemption from any tax upon real property shall be granted by the General Assembly under this clause unless the General Assembly shall provide for the reimbursement of local taxing authorities by or through the Commonwealth for revenue losses occasioned by such exemption;

    (iii) Establish standards and qualifications by which local taxing authorities may make uniform special tax provisions applicable to a taxpayer for a limited period of time to encourage improvement of deteriorating property or areas by an individual, association or corporation, or to encourage industrial development by a non-profit corporation; and

    (iv) Make special tax provisions on any increase in value of real estate resulting from residential construction. Such special tax provisions shall be applicable for a period not to exceed two years.

    (c) Citizens and residents of this Commonwealth, who served in any war or armed conflict in which the United States was engaged and were honorably discharged or released under honorable circumstances from active service, shall be exempt from the payment of all real property taxes upon the residence occupied by the said citizens and residents of this Commonwealth imposed by the Commonwealth of Pennsylvania or any of its political subdivisions if, as a result of military service, they are blind, paraplegic or double or quadruple amputees, and if the State Veteran's Commission determines that such persons are in need of the tax exemptions granted herein.

Art. VIII, § 4. The real property of public utilities is subject to real estate taxes imposed by local taxing authorities. Payment to the Commonwealth of gross receipts taxes or other special taxes in replacement of gross receipts taxes by a public utility and the distribution by the Commonwealth to the local taxing authorities of the amount as herein provided shall, however, be in lieu of local taxes upon its real property which is used or useful in furnishing its public utility service. The amount raised annually by such gross receipts or other special taxes shall not be less than the gross amount of real estate taxes which the local taxing authorities could have imposed upon such real property but for the exemption herein provided. This gross amount shall be determined in the manner provided by law. . . .

Notwithstanding the provisions of this section, any law which presently subjects real property of public utilities to local real estate taxation by local taxing authorities shall remain in full force and effect.

Art. VIII, § 5. All laws exempting property from taxation, other than the property above enumerated shall be void.

Art. VIII, § 6. The power to tax corporations and corporate property shall not be surrendered or suspended by any contract or grant to which the Commonwealth shall be a party.

Puerto Rico Constitution (1952)[a]

Art. VI, § 2. The power of the Commonwealth of Puerto Rico to impose and collect taxes and to authorize their imposition and collection by municipalities shall be exercised as determined by the Legislative Assembly and shall never be surrendered or suspended. . . .

Art. VI, § 3. The rule of taxation in Puerto Rico shall be uniform.

---

[a] The constitution was signed February 6, 1952; adopted by Puerto Rico, March 3, 1952; U.S. Congressional approval, July 3, 1953, P.L. 447, 82nd Cong.; proclaimed, July 25, 1952. Commonwealth status is established by compact with the United States. Reference should be made to the Organic Act of March 2, 1917, c. 145, 39 Stat. 951 and P.L. 600, 81st Cong., Act of July 3, 1950, c. 446, 64 Stat. 320, known as the Puerto Rico Federal Relations Act. The preceding constitutional tax provisions were also to be found in the Organic Act. In addition, § 3 of the Federal Relations Act contains the following provision: ". . . taxes and assessments on property, income taxes, internal revenue, and license fees, and royalties for franchises, privileges, and concessions may be imposed for the purposes of the insular and municipal governments, respectively, as may be provided and defined by the Legislature of Puerto Rico. . . ."

Rhode Island Constitution (1843)

Art. I, § 2. All free governments are instituted for the protection, safety and happiness of the people. All laws, therefore, should be made for the good of the whole; and the burdens of the state ought to be fairly distributed among its citizens.

Art. IV, § 15. The general assembly shall, from time to time, provide for making new valuations of property, for the assessment of taxes, in such manner as they may deem best. . . .

South Carolina Constitution (1895. Renumbered 1977)

Art. III, § 29. Taxes laid upon actual assessed value.—All taxes upon property, real and personal, shall be laid upon the actual value of the property taxed, as the same shall be ascertained by an assessment made for the purpose of laying such tax.

Art. X, § 1. The General Assembly may provide for the ad valorem taxation by the State or any of its subdivisions of all real and personal property. The assessment of all property shall be equal and uniform in the following classifications:

(1) All real and personal property owned by or leased to manufacturers, utilities and mining operations and used by the manufacturer, utility or mining operation, in the conduct of such business shall be taxed on an assessment equal to ten and one-half percent of the fair market value of such property.

(2) All real and personal property owned by or leased to companies primarily engaged in transportation for hire of persons or property and used by the company in the conduct of such business shall be taxed on an assessment equal to nine and one-half percent of the fair market value of such property.

(3) The legal residence and not more than five acres contiguous thereto shall be taxed on an assessment equal to four percent of the fair market value of such property.

(4) Agricultural real property which is actually used for such purposes shall be taxed on an assessment equal to:

(A) four percent of its value for such purposes when owned or leased to individuals or partnerships and certain corporations. . . .

(B) six percent of its value for such purposes when owned or leased to corporations, except for certain corporations specified in (A) above.

Provided, that the General Assembly shall by general law provide for a penalty system on lands classified as agricultural lands to insure the proper utilization of this classification.

(5) All other real property not herein provided for shall be taxed on an assessment equal to six percent of the fair market value of such property. . . .

Art. X, § 2. (a) The General Assembly may define the classes of property and values for property tax purposes of the classes of property set forth in Section 1 of this article and establish administrative procedures for property owners to qualify for a particular classification.

(b) The General Assembly may provide for a gradual transition to any ratio as set out in Section 1 over a period not to exceed seven years.

(c) Statutes pertaining to the methods of assessment of property for ad valorem taxation not in conflict with this article shall continue in force until changed by an act of the General Assembly.

(d) The General Assembly may change the ratios as set forth in Section 1, but only with the approval of at least two-thirds of the membership of each house.

Art. X, § 3. There shall be exempt from ad valorem taxation:

(a) all property of the State, counties, municipalities, school districts and other political subdivisions, if the property is used exclusively for public purposes;

(b) all property of all schools, colleges and other institutions of learning and all charitable institutions in the nature of hospitals and institutions caring for the infirmed, the handicapped, the aged, children and indigent persons, except where the profits of such institutions are applied to private use;

(c) all property of all public libraries, churches, parsonages and burying grounds;

(d) all property of all charitable trusts and foundations used exclusively for charitable and public purposes. . . .

(g) all new manufacturing establishments located in any of the counties of this State after July 1, 1977, for five years from the time of establishment and all additions to the existing manufacturing establishments located in any of the counties of this State for five years from the time each such addition is made if the cost of such addition is fifty thousand dollars or more. Such additions shall include additional machinery and equipment installed in the plant. Provided, however, that the exemptions authorized in this item for manufacturing establishments, and additions thereto shall not include exemptions from school taxes or municipal taxes but shall include only county taxes. Provided, further, that all manufacturing establishments and all additions to existing manufacturing establishments exempt under existing statutes shall be allowed their exemptions provided for by statute until such exemptions expire;

(h) all facilities or equipment of industrial plants which are designed for the elimination, mitigation, prevention, treatment, abatement or control of water, air or noise pollution;

(i) a homestead exemption for persons sixty-five years of age and older, for persons permanently and totally disabled and for blind persons in the amount of ten thousand dollars of the fair market value of the homestead under conditions prescribed by the General Assembly by general law; provided, that the amount may be increased by the General Assembly by general law, passed by a majority vote of both houses;

(j) intangible personal property.

The exemptions provided in subitems (c) and (d) for real property shall not extend beyond the buildings and premises actually occupied by the owners of such real property.

Homestead exemptions from ad valorem taxation not specifically provided for in this section may be provided for by the General Assembly by general law.

In addition to the exemptions listed in this section, the General Assembly may provide for exemptions from the property tax, by general laws applicable uniformly to property throughout the State and in all political subdivisions, but only with the approval of two-thirds of the members of each House.

All exemptions not specifically provided for or authorized in this article shall be repealed March 1, 1978.

The General Assembly shall provide for methods and procedures in applying for the exemption of any property as is described in this section.

Art. X, § 4. The General Assembly shall provide for the assessment of all property for taxation, whether for state, county, school, municipal or any other political subdivision. All taxes shall be levied on that assessment.

Art. X, § 5. No tax, subsidy or charge shall be established, fixed, laid or levied, under any pretext whatsoever, without the consent of the people or their representatives lawfully assembled. Any tax which shall be levied shall distinctly state the public purpose to which the proceeds of the tax shall be applied.

Art. X, § 6. The General Assembly may vest the power of assessment and collecting taxes in all of the political subdivisions of the State. Property tax levies shall be uniform in respect to persons and property within the jurisdiction of the body imposing such taxes; provided, that on properties located in an area receiving special benefits from the taxes collected, special levies may be permitted by general law applicable to the same type of political subdivision throughout the State, and the General Assembly shall specify the precise condition under which such special levies shall be assessed.

Whenever there is a merger of governments . . . tax districts may be created, based upon the services rendered in each district, but tax levies must be uniform in respect to persons and property within each such district.

Art. XIV, § 4. Navigable waters free; tax for use of wharf.—All navigable waters shall forever remain public highways free to the citizens of the State and the United States without tax, impost or toll imposed; and no tax, toll, impost or wharfage shall be imposed, demanded or received from the owners of any merchandise or commodity for the use of the shores or any wharf erected on the shores or in or over the waters of any navigable stream unless the same be authorized by the General Assembly.

South Dakota Constitution (1889)

Art. III, § 26. The legislature shall not delegate to any special commission, private corporation or association, any power to ... levy taxes ... or to perform any municipal functions whatever.

Art. VI, § 17. [Taxation.]
No tax or duty shall be imposed without the consent of the people or their representatives in the legislature, and all taxation shall be equal and uniform.

Art. VIII, § 15. [School Taxes.]
The Legislature shall make such provision by general taxation and by authorizing the school corporations to levy such additional taxes as with the income from the permanent school fund shall secure a thorough and efficient system of common schools throughout the state. The Legislature is empowered to classify properties within school districts for purposes of school taxation, and may constitute agricultural property a separate class. Taxes shall be uniform on all property in the same class.

Art. XI, § 1. The legislature shall provide for an annual tax, sufficient to defray the estimated ordinary expenses of the state for each year, not to exceed in any one year two mills on each dollar of the assessed valuation of all taxable property in the state, to be ascertained by the last assessment made for state and county purposes.
. . . .

Art. XI, § 2. [Classification of Property.]
To the end that the burden of taxation may be equitable upon all property, and in order that no property which is made subject to taxation shall escape, the legislature is empowered to divide all property including moneys and credits as well as physical property into classes and to determine what class or classes of property shall be subject to taxation and what property, if any, shall not be subject to taxation. Taxes shall be uniform on all property of the same class, and shall be levied and collected for public purposes only. Taxes may be imposed upon any and all property including privileges, franchises and licenses to do business in the state. Gross earnings and net incomes may be considered in taxing any and all property and the valuation of property for taxation purposes shall never exceed the actual value thereof. The legislature is empowered to impose taxes upon incomes and occupations, and taxes upon incomes may be graduated and progressive and reasonable exemptions may be provided.

Art. XI, § 3. [Taxation of Corporations.]
The power to tax corporations and corporate property shall not be surrendered or suspended by any contract or grant to which the state shall be a party.

Art. XI, § 5. [Exemption of Public Property.]
The property of the United States and the state, county and municipal corporations, both real and personal, shall be exempt from taxation, provided, however, that all state owned lands acquired under the provisions of the rural credit act may be taxed by the local taxing districts for county, township and school purposes. . . .

Art. XI, § 6. [Exemption of Private Property.]
The legislature shall, by general law, exempt from taxation, property used exclusively for agricultural and horticultural societies, for school, religious, cemetery and charitable purposes, property acquired and used exclusively for public highway purposes. . . .

Art. XI, § 7. [Other Tax Exemptions.]
All laws exempting property from taxation other than that enumerated in sections 5 and 6 of this article, shall be void.

Art. XI, § 10. [Local Improvements.]
The legislature may vest the corporate authority of cities, towns and villages, with power to make local improvements by special taxation of contiguous property or otherwise. For all corporate purposes, all municipal corporations may be vested with authority to assess and collect taxes; but such tax shall be uniform in respect to persons and property within the jurisdiction of the body levying the same.

(Note: A new section was added to art. XI in November 1978. See appendix B.)

Art. XXII. . . . Second . . . lands belonging to citizens of the United States residing without the said state shall never be taxed at a higher rate than the lands belonging to residents of this state; . . . no taxes shall be imposed by the state of South Dakota on lands or property therein belonging to or which thereafter be purchased by the United States, or reserved for its use. . . .[a]

---

[a]This clause is similar to that found in art. XXVI, § 18. *Ordinances.* (Second.) and is not repeated herein.

Tennessee Constitution (1870)

Art. II, § 28. Taxable property—Valuation—Rates.—In accordance with the following provisions, all property real, personal or mixed shall be subject to taxation, but the Legislature may except such as may be held by the State, by Counties, Cities or Towns, and used exclusively for public or corporation purposes, and such as may be held and used for purposes purely religious, charitable, scientific, literary or educational, and shall except the direct product of the soil in the hands of the producer, and his immediate vendee. . . . For purposes of taxation, property shall be classified into three classes, to wit: Real Property, Tangible Personal Property and Intangible Personal Property.

Real Property shall be classified into four (4) subclassifications and assessed as follows:

    (a) Public Utility Property, to be assessed at fifty-five (55%) per cent of its value;

    (b) Industrial and Commercial Property, to be assessed at forty (40%) per cent of its value;

    (c) Residential Property, to be assessed at twenty-five (25%) per cent of its value, provided that residential property containing two (2) or more rental units is hereby defined as industrial and commercial property; and

    (d) Farm Property, to be assessed at twenty-five (25%) per cent of its value.

House trailers, mobile homes, and all other similar movable structures used for commercial, industrial, or residential purposes shall be assessed as Real Property as an improvement to the land where located.

The Legislature shall provide tax relief to elderly low-income taxpayers through payments by the State to reimburse all or part of the taxes paid by such persons on owner-occupied residential property, but such reimbursement shall not be an obligation imposed, directly or indirectly, upon Counties, Cities or Towns . . . provided further, that such relief shall not extend to persons having a total annual income from all sources in excess of Four Thousand Eight Hundred ($4,800) Dollars.

The Legislature may provide tax relief to home owners totally and permanently disabled, irrespective of age, as provided herein for the elderly. . . .

The ratio of assessment to value of property in each class or sub-class shall be equal and uniform throughout the State, the value and definition of property in each class or subclass to be ascertained in such manner as the Legislature shall direct. Each respective taxing authority shall apply the same tax rate to all property within its jurisdiction.

The Legislature shall have power to tax . . . privileges, in such manner as they may from time to time direct . . . . The Legislature shall have power to levy a tax upon incomes derived from stocks and bonds that are not taxed ad valorem.

Art. II, § 29. The General Assembly shall have power to authorize the several counties and incorporated towns of this State, to impose taxes for County and Corporation purposes respectively, in such manner as shall be prescribed by law; and all property shall be taxed according to its value, upon the principles established in regard to state taxation. . . .

Art. XI, § 9. . . . The General Assembly shall not authorize any municipality to tax incomes, estates, or inheritances, or to impose any other tax not authorized by Sections 28 or 29 of Article II of this Constitution. Nothing herein shall be construed as invalidating the provisions of any municipal charter in existence at the time of the adoption of this amendment.

. . . .

Texas Constitution (1876)

Art. III, § 56. The Legislature shall not, except as otherwise provided in this Constitution, pass any local or special law authorizing:

. . . .

Exempting property from taxation;

. . . .

Extending the time for the assessment or collection of taxes. . . .

Art. VIII,[a] § 1. **Taxation to Be Equal and Uniform; Occupation and Income Taxes; Exemptions; Limitations Upon Counties, Cities, Etc.** —Taxation shall be equal and uniform. All property in this State, whether owned by natural persons or corporations, other than municipal, shall be taxed in proportion to its value, which shall be ascertained as may be provided by law. The Legislature may impose . . . occupation taxes, both upon natural persons and upon corporations, other than municipal, doing any business in this State. It may also tax incomes of both natural persons and corporations, other than municipal, except that persons engaged in mechanical and agricultural pursuits shall never be required to pay an occupation tax . . . and provided, further, that the occupation tax levied by any county, city or town, for any year, on persons or corporations pursuing any profession or business, shall not exceed one-half of the tax levied by the State for the same period on such profession or business.

Art. VIII, § 1-a. From and after January 1, 1951, no State ad valorem tax shall be levied upon any property within this State for general revenue purposes. From and after January 1, 1951, the several counties of the State are authorized to levy ad valorem taxes upon all property within their respective boundaries for county purposes, except the first three thousand dollars ($3,000) value of residential homesteads, not to exceed thirty cents (30¢) on each one hundred dollars ($100) valuation, in addition to all other ad valorem taxes authorized by the Constitution of this State, provided the revenue derived therefrom shall be used for construction and maintenance of farm-to-market roads or for flood control, except as herein otherwise provided.

. . . .

Art. VIII, § 1-b. **Homestead Exemption Under State Tax.** —(a) Three Thousand dollars ($3,000) of the assessed taxable value of all residence homesteads as now defined by law shall be exempt from all taxation for all State purposes. (b) From and after January 1, 1973, the governing body of any county, city, town, school

---

[a] Art. VIII of the constitution has been extensively amended November 1978. See appendix B.

district, or other political subdivision of the State may exempt by its own action not less than three thousand dollars ($3,000) of the assessed value of residence homesteads of persons sixty-five (65) years of age or older from all ad valorem taxes thereafter levied by the political subdivision....

Art. VIII, § 1-d. Taxation of Agricultural Land.—(a) All land owned by natural persons which is designated for agricultural use in accordance with the provisions of this section shall be assessed for all tax purposes on the consideration of only those factors relative to such agricultural use. "Agricultural use" means the raising of livestock or growing of crops, fruit, flowers, and other products of the soil under natural conditions as a business venture for profit, which business is the primary occupation and source of income of the owner.

....

(g) The valuation and assessment of any minerals or subsurface rights to minerals shall not come with the provisions of this section.

Art. VIII, § 1-e. (1) Gradual Abolition of Ad Valorem Tax.—From and after December 31, 1978, no State ad valorem taxes shall be levied upon any property within this State for State purposes except the tax levied ... for certain institutions of higher learning.

Art. VIII, § 2. (a) All occupation taxes shall be equal and uniform upon the same class of subjects within the limits of the authority levying the tax; but the Legislature may, by general laws, exempt from taxation public property used for public purposes; actual places of religious worship ... places of burial not held for private or corporate profit;[a] all buildings used exclusively and owned by persons or associations of persons for school purposes ... and institutions of purely public charity; and all laws exempting property from taxation other than the property mentioned in this Section shall be null and void.

(b) The Legislature may, by general law, exempt property owned by a disabled veteran or by the surviving spouse and surviving minor children of a disabled veteran ... [may be granted exemptions of up to $3,000]

Art. VIII, § 4. Power to Tax Corporations Not to Be Surrendered.—The power to tax corporations and corporate property shall not be surrendered or suspended by act of the Legislature, by any contract or grant to which the State shall be a party.

Art. VIII, § 5. Railroad Taxes Due Cities and Towns.—All property of railroad companies, of whatever description lying or being within the limits of any city or incorporated town within this State, shall bear its proportionate share of municipal taxation, and if any such property shall not have been heretofore

---

[a] A November 1978 amendment added the words: "solar or wind powered energy devices;" at this point.

rendered, the authorities of the city or town within which it lies shall have power to require its rendition and collect the usual municipal tax thereon, as on other property lying within said municipality.

Art. VIII, § 8. Railroad Property; How Assessed.—All property of railroad companies shall be assessed, and the taxes collected in the several counties in which said property is situated, including so much of the roadbed and fixtures as shall be in each county. The rolling stock may be assessed in gross in the county where the principal office of the company is located, and the county tax paid upon it shall be apportioned by the Comptroller, in proportion to the distance such road may run through any such county, among the several counties through which the road passes, as part of their tax assets.

Art. VIII, § 9. The State tax on property, exclusive of the tax necessary to pay the public debt, and of the taxes provided for the benefit of the public free school, shall never exceed thirty-five cents (35¢) on the One Hundred Dollars ($100) valuation; and no county, city or town shall levy a tax rate in excess of Eighty Cents (80¢) on the One Hundred Dollars ($100) valuation in any one (1) year for general fund, permanent improvement fund, road and bridge fund and jury fund purposes. . . . This section shall not be construed as a limitation of powers delegated to counties, cities or towns by any other section or sections of this Constitution.

Art. VIII, § 17. Power of Legislature as to Taxes.—The specification of the objects and subjects of taxation shall not deprive the Legislature of the power to require other subjects or objects to be taxed, in such manner as may be consistent with the principles of taxation fixed in this Constitution.

Art. VIII, § 18. Equalization of Taxes. The Legislature shall provide for equalizing, as near as may be, the valuation of all property subject to or rendered for taxation (the County Commissioners' Court to constitute a board of equalization); and may also provide for the classification of all lands with reference to their value in the several counties.

Art. VIII, § 20. No property of any kind in this State shall ever be assessed for ad valorem taxes at a greater value than its fair cash market value nor shall any Board of Equalization of any governmental or political subdivision or taxing district within this State fix the value of any property for tax purposes at more than its fair cash market value. . . .

Art. XI, § 4. Cities and towns having a population of 5,000 or less may be chartered alone by general laws. They may levy, assess and collect such taxes as may be authorized by law, but no tax for any purpose shall ever be lawful for any one year which shall exceed 1 per cent of the taxable property of such city. . . .

Art. XI, § 5. Cities having more than five thousand (5,000) inhabitants may, by a majority vote of the qualified voters of said city, at an election held for that purpose, adopt or amend their charters, subject to such limitations as may be prescribed by the Legislature, and providing that no charter or any ordinance passed under said charter shall contain any provision inconsistent with the Constitution of the State or of the general laws enacted by the Legislature of this State; said cities may levy, assess and collect such taxes as may be authorized by law or by their charters; but no tax for any purpose shall ever be lawful for any one year which shall exceed 2½ per cent of the taxable property of such city. . . .

Art. XI, § 9. The property of counties, cities and towns owned and held only for public purposes, such as public buildings and the sites therefor . . . public grounds and all other property devoted exclusively to the use and benefit of the public, shall be exempt from . . . taxation. . . .

Utah Constitution (1896)

Art. III ORDINANCE ... Second.... The lands belonging to citizens of the United States, residing without this State shall never be taxed at a higher rate than the lands belonging to residents of this State....

Art. XI, § 5. ... Each city forming its charter under this section shall have, and is hereby granted, the authority to exercise all powers relating to municipal affairs....

The power to be conferred upon the cities by this section shall include the following:

(a) To levy, assess and collect taxes and borrow money, within the limits prescribed by general law, and to levy and collect special assessments for benefits conferred.

....

Art. XIII, § 2. All tangible property in the state, not exempt under the laws of the United States, or under this constitution, shall be taxed in proportion to its value, to be ascertained as provided by law. The property of the state, counties, cities, towns, school districts, municipal corporations and public libraries, lots with the buildings thereon used exclusively for either religious worship or charitable purposes, and places of burial not held or used for private or corporate benefit, shall be exempt from taxation.... Water rights, ditches, canals, reservoirs, power plants, pumping plants, transmission lines, pipes and flumes owned and used by individuals or corporations for irrigating land within the state owned by such individuals or corporations, or the individual members thereof, shall not be separately taxed so long as they shall be owned and used exclusively for such purposes. Power plants, power transmission lines and other property used for generating and delivering electrical power, a portion of which is used for furnishing power for pumping water for irrigation purposes on lands in the state of Utah, may be exempted from taxation to the extent that such property is used for such purposes.... The legislature may provide for the exemption from taxation of homes, homesteads, and personal property, not to exceed $2,000 in value for homes, homesteads, and all household furnishings.... Property not to exceed $3,000 in value, owned by disabled persons who served in any war in the military service of the United States or the state of Utah and by the unmarried widows and minor orphans of such disabled persons or of persons who while serving in the military service of the United States or the state of Utah were killed in action or died as a result of such service may be exempted as the legislature may provide....

Art. XIII, §3. The Legislature shall provide by law a uniform and equal rate of assessment and taxation on all tangible property in the State according to its value in money, and shall prescribe by law such regulations as shall secure a just valuation for taxation of such property, so that every person and corporation shall pay a tax in proportion to the value of his, her, or its tangible property. . . . Land used for agricultural purposes may, as the Legislature prescribes, be assessed according to its value for agricultural use without regard to the value it may have for other purposes. Intangible property may be exempted from taxation as property or it may be taxed in such manner and to such extent as the Legislature may provide. Provided that if intangible property be taxed as property the rate thereof shall not exceed five mills on each dollar valuation. When exempted from taxation as property, the taxable income therefrom shall be taxed under any tax based on incomes, but when taxed by the State of Utah as property, the income therefrom shall not also be taxed. The Legislature may provide for deductions, exemptions, and/or offsets on any tax based upon income. The personal income tax rates shall be graduated but the maximum rate shall not exceed six percent of net income. No excise tax rate based upon income shall exceed four percent of net income. . . .

Art. XIII, § 4. All metalliferous mines or mining claims, both placer and rock in place, shall be assessed as the Legislature shall provide. . . . All other mines or mining claims and other valuable mineral deposits, including lands containing coal or hydrocarbons and all machinery used in mining and all property or surface improvements upon or appurtenant to mines or mining claims, and the value of any surface use made of mining claims, or mining property for other than mining purposes, shall be assessed as other tangible property.

Art. XIII, § 5. The Legislature shall not impose taxes for the purpose of any county, city, town or other municipal corporation, but may, by law, vest in the corporate authorities thereof, respectively, the power to assess and collect taxes for all purposes of such corporation.

Art. XIII, § 7. The rate of taxation on tangible property shall not exceed on each dollar of valuation, two and four-tenths mills for general State purposes, and such additional levy as the Legislature may provide for the State's share of the support of a portion of the public school system. . . .

Art. XIII, § 12. Nothing in this constitution shall be construed to prevent the Legislature from providing a stamp tax, or a tax based on income, occupation, licenses or franchises.

Art. XIV, § 8. The legislature by general law may authorize any county, city, or town to establish special districts within all or any part of the county, city, or town to be governed by the governing authority of the county, city, or town with power to provide water, sewerage, drainage, flood control, garbage, hospital, transportation, recreation, and fire protection services or any combination of these services and may authorize the county, city, or town: (1) to levy taxes upon the taxable property in only such districts for the purpose of acquiring, constructing, equipping, operating, and maintaining facilities required for any or all of these services. . . .

Vermont Constitution (1793)

Ch. I, Art. 9th. That every member of society hath a right to be protected in the enjoyment of life, liberty, and property, and therefore is bound to contribute his proportion towards the expence of that protection . . . and previous to any law being made to raise a tax, the purpose for which it is to be raised ought to appear evident to the Legislature to be of more service to community than the money would be if not collected.

Virginia Constitution (1971)

Art. I, § 6. ... all men, having sufficient evidence of permanent common interest with, and attachment to, the community, have the right of suffrage, and cannot be taxed, or deprived of, or damaged in, their property for public uses, without their own consent, or that of their representatives duly elected, or bound by any law to which they have not, in like manner, assented for the public good.

Art. IV, § 14. ... The General Assembly shall not enact any local, special, or private law in the following cases:

. . . .

(5) For the assessment and collection of taxes, except as to animals which the General Assembly may deem dangerous to the farming interests.

(6) Extending the time for the assessment or collection of taxes.

(7) Exempting property from taxation.

. . . .

Art. IV, § 15. ... No general or special law shall surrender or suspend the right and power of the Commonwealth, or any political subdivision thereof, to tax corporations and corporate property, except as authorized by Article X. . . .

Art. VII, § 2. ... The General Assembly may also provide by special act for the organization, government, and powers of any county, city, town, or regional government, including such powers of legislation, taxation, and assessment as the General Assembly may determine, but no such special act shall be adopted which provides for the extension or contraction of boundaries of any county, city or town.

. . . .

Art. X, § 1. Taxable property; uniformity; classification and segregation.

All property, except as hereinafter provided, shall be taxed. All taxes shall be levied and collected under general laws and shall be uniform upon the same class of subjects within the territorial limits of the authority levying the tax, except that the General Assembly may provide for differences in the rate of taxation to be imposed upon real estate by a city or town within all or parts of areas added to its territorial limits, or by a new unit of general government, within its area, created by or encompassing two or more, or parts of two or more, existing units of general government. Such differences in the rate of taxation shall bear a reasonable relationship to differences between nonrevenue producing governmental services giving land urban character which are furnished in one or several areas in contrast to the services furnished in other areas of such unit of government.

The General Assembly may define and classify taxable subjects. Except as to classes of property herein expressly segregated for either State or local taxation, the General Assembly may segregate the several classes of property so as to specify and determine upon what subjects State taxes, and upon what subjects local taxes, may be levied.

Art. X, § 2. Assessments.

All assessments of real estate and tangible personal property shall be at their fair market value, to be ascertained as prescribed by law. The General Assembly may define and classify real estate devoted to agricultural, horticultural, forest, or open space uses, and may by general law authorize any county, city, town, or regional government to allow deferral of, or relief from, portions of taxes otherwise payable on such real estate if it were not so classified, provided the General Assembly shall first determine that classification of such real estate for such purpose is in the public interest for the preservation or conservation of real estate for such uses. In the event the General Assembly defines and classifies real estate for such purposes, it shall prescribe the limits, conditions, and extent of such deferral or relief. No such deferral or relief shall be granted within the territorial limits of any county, city, town, or regional government except by ordinance adopted by the governing body thereof.

So long as the Commonwealth shall levy upon any public service corporation a State franchise, license, or other similar tax based upon or measured by its gross receipts or gross earnings, or any part thereof, its real estate and tangible personal property shall be assessed by a central State agency, as prescribed by law.

Art. X, § 3. Taxes or assessments upon abutting property owners.

The General Assembly by general law may authorize any county, city, town, or regional government to impose taxes or assessments upon abutting property owners for such local public improvements as may be designated by the General Assembly; however, such taxes or assessments shall not be in excess of the peculiar benefits resulting from the improvements to such abutting property owners.

Art. X, § 4. Property segregated for local taxation; exceptions.

Real estate, coal and other mineral lands, and tangible personal property, except the rolling stock of public service corporations, are hereby segregated for, and made subject to, local taxation only, and shall be assessed for local taxation in such manner and at such times as the General Assembly may prescribe by general law.

Art. X, § 5. The General Assembly, in imposing a franchise tax upon corporations, may in its discretion make the same in lieu of taxes upon other property, in whole or in part, of such corporations. . . .

Art. X, § 6. Exempt property.[a]

(a) Except as otherwise provided in this Constitution, the following property and no other shall be exempt from taxation, State and local, including inheritance taxes:

(1) Property owned directly or indirectly by the Commonwealth or any political subdivision thereof, and obligations of the Commonwealth or any political subdivision thereof exempt by law.

(2) Real estate and personal property owned and exclusively occupied or used by churches or religious bodies for religious worship or for the residences of their ministers.

(3) Private or public burying grounds or cemeteries, provided the same are not operated for profit.

(4) Property owned by public libraries or by institutions of learning not conducted for profit, so long as such property is primarily used for literary, scientific, or educational purposes or purposes incidental thereto. This provision may also apply to leasehold interests in such property as may be provided by general law.

(5) Intangible personal property, or any class or classes thereof, as may be exempted in whole or in part by general law.

(6) Property used by its owner for religious, charitable, patriotic, historical, benevolent, cultural, or public park and playground purposes, as may be provided by classification or designation by a three-fourths vote of the members elected to each house of the General Assembly and subject to such restrictions and conditions as may be prescribed.

(7) Land subject to a perpetual easement permitting inundation by water as may be exempted in whole or in part by general law.

(b) The General Assembly may by general law authorize the governing body of any county, city, town, or regional government to provide for the exemption from local real property taxation, or a portion thereof, within such restrictions and upon such conditions as may be prescribed, of real estate owned by, and occupied as the sole dwelling of, persons not less than sixty-five years of age or persons permanently and totally disabled as established by general law who are deemed by the General Assembly to be bearing an extraordinary tax burden on said real estate in relation to their income and financial worth.

(c) Except as to property of the Commonwealth, the General Assembly by general law may restrict or condition, in whole or in part, but not extend, any or all of the above exemptions.

---

[a]Art. X, § 6 has been amended by adding a new paragraph (h), November 1978. See appendix B.

(d) The General Assembly may define as a separate subject of taxation any property, including real or personal property, equipment, facilities, or devices, used primarily for the purpose of abating or preventing pollution of the atmosphere or waters of the Commonwealth or for the purpose of transferring or storing solar energy, and by general law may allow the governing body of any county, city, town, or regional government to exempt or partially exempt such property from taxation, or by general law may directly exempt or partially exempt such property from taxation.

(e) The General Assembly may define as a separate subject of taxation household goods, personal effects and tangible farm property and products, and by general law may allow the governing body of any county, city, town, or regional government to exempt or partially exempt such property from taxation, or by general law may directly exempt or partially exempt such property from taxation.

(f) Exemptions of property from taxation as established or authorized hereby shall be strictly construed; provided, however, that all property exempt from taxation on the effective date of this section shall continue to be exempt until otherwise provided by the General Assembly as herein set forth.

(g) The General Assembly may by general law authorize any county, city, town, or regional government to impose a service charge upon the owners of a class or classes of exempt property for services provided by such governments.

Art. X, § 8. Limit of tax or revenue.

No other or greater amount of tax or revenues shall, at any time, be levied than may be required for the necessary expenses of the government, or to pay the indebtedness of the Commonwealth.

Washington Constitution (1889)

Art. VII, § 1. Taxation.—The power of taxation shall never be suspended, surrendered or contracted away. All taxes shall be uniform upon the same class of property within the territorial limits of the authority levying the tax and shall be levied, and collected for public purposes only. The word "property" as used herein shall mean and include everything, whether tangible or intangible, subject to ownership. All real estate shall constitute one class: Provided, That the legislature may tax mines and mineral resources and lands devoted to reforestation by either a yield tax or ad valorem tax at such rate as it may fix, or by both. Such property as the legislature may by general laws provide shall be exempt from taxation. Property of the United States and of the state, counties, school districts and other municipal corporations, and credits secured by property actually taxed in this state, not exceeding in value the value of such property, shall be exempt from taxation. The legislature shall have power, by appropriate legislation, to exempt personal property to the amount of three hundred ($300.00) dollars for each head of a family liable to assessment and taxation under the provisions of the laws of this state of which the individual is the actual bona fide owner.

Art. VII, § 2. Except as hereinafter provided and notwithstanding any other provision of this Constitution, the aggregate of all tax levies upon real and personal property by the state and all taxing districts now existing or hereafter created, shall not in any year exceed one per centum of the true and fair value of such property in money: PROVIDED, HOWEVER, That nothing herein shall prevent levies at the rates now provided by law by or for any port or public utility district. . . .

Art. VII, § 3. Taxation of Federal Agencies and Property.—The United States and its agencies and instrumentalites, and their property, may be taxed under any of the tax laws of this state, whenever and in such manner as such taxation may be authorized or permitted under the laws of the United States, notwithstanding anything to the contrary in the Constitution of this state.

Art. VII, § 5. Taxes, How Levied.—No tax shall be levied except in pursuance of law; and every law imposing a tax shall state distinctly the object of the same to which only it shall be applied.

Art. VII, § 9. Special Assessments or Taxation for Local Improvements.—The legislature may vest the corporate authorities of cities, towns and villages with power to make local improvements by special assessment, or by special taxation of property benefited. For all corporate purposes, all municipal corporations may be vested with authority to assess and collect taxes and such taxes shall be uniform in respect to persons and property within the jurisdiction of the body levying the same.

Art. VII, § 10. ... The legislature shall have the power, by appropriate legislation, to grant to retired property owners relief from the property tax on the real property occupied as a residence by those owners. The legislature may place such restrictions and conditions upon the granting of such relief as it shall deem proper. Such restrictions and conditions may include, but are not limited to, the limiting of the relief of those property owners below a specific level of income and those fulfilling certain minimum residential requirements.

Art. VII, § 11. Taxation Based on Actual Use.—Nothing in this Article VII as amended shall prevent the legislature from providing, subject to such conditions as it may enact, that the true and fair value in money (a) of farms, agricultural lands, standing timber and timberlands, and (b) of other open space lands which are used for recreation or for enjoyment of their scenic or natural beauty shall be based on the use to which such property is currently applied, and such values shall be used in computing the assessed valuation of such property in the same manner as the assessed valuation is computed for all property.

Art. XI, § 9. State Taxes Not to Be Released or Commuted.—No county, nor the inhabitants thereof, nor the property therein, shall be released or discharged from its or their proportionate share of taxes to be levied for state purposes, nor shall commutation for such taxes be authorized in any form whatever.

Art. XI, § 12. Assessment and Collection of Taxes in Municipalities.—The legislature shall have no power to impose taxes upon counties, cities, towns or other municipal corporations, or upon the inhabitants or property thereof, for county, city, town or other municipal purposes, but may, by general laws, vest in the corporate authorities thereof, the power to assess and collect taxes for such purposes.

Art. XI, § 16. The legislature shall, by general law, provide for the formation of combined city and county municipal corporations, and for the manner of determining the territorial limits thereof, each of which shall be known as a "city and county," and when organized, shall contain a population of at least three hundred thousand (300,000) inhabitants. ...

No county or county government existing outside the territorial limits of such county and city shall exercise any police, taxation or other powers within the territorial limits of such county and city, but all such powers shall be exercised by the city and county and the officers thereof, subject to such constitutional provisions and general laws as apply to either cities or counties. ...

Art. XXVI –COMPACT WITH THE UNITED STATES

The following ordinance shall be irrevocable without the consent of the United States and the people of this state: —

Second. . . . lands belonging to citizens of the United States residing without the limits of this state shall never be taxed at a higher rate than the lands belonging to residents thereof; and . . . no taxes shall be imposed by the state on lands or property therein, belonging to or which may be hereafter purchased by the United States or reserved for use. . . .

West Virginia Constitution (1872)

Art. VI, § 39. The Legislature shall not pass local or special laws in any of the following enumerated cases; that is to say, for

. . . .

Releasing taxes. . . .

Art. VI, § 39-a. No local or special law shall hereafter be passed incorporating cities, towns or villages, or amending their charters. . . . General laws shall restrict the powers of such cities, towns and villages . . . and shall limit the rate of taxes for municipal purposes, in accordance with section one, article ten of the Constitution of the State of West Virginia. . . .

Art. VI, § 53. The Legislature may by general law define and classify forest lands and provide for cooperation by contract between the State and the owner in the planting, protection, and harvesting thereof. Forest lands embraced in any such contract may be exempted from all taxation or be taxed in such manner, including the imposition of a severance tax or charge as trees are harvested, as the Legislature may from time to time provide. But any tax measured by valuation shall not exceed the aggregate rates authorized by section one of article ten of this Constitution.

Art. X, § 1. Subject to the exceptions in this section contained, taxation shall be equal and uniform throughout the State, and all property, both real and personal, shall be taxed in proportion to its value to be ascertained as directed by law. No one species of property from which a tax may be collected shall be taxed higher than any other species of property of equal value; except that the aggregate of taxes assessed in any one year upon personal property employed exclusively in agriculture, including horticulture and grazing, products of agriculture as above defined, including livestock, while owned by the producer . . . shall not exceed fifty cents on each one hundred dollars of value thereon and upon all property owned, used and occupied by the owner thereof exclusively for residential purposes and upon farms occupied and cultivated by their owners or bona fide tenants, one dollar; and upon all other property situated outside of municipalities, one dollar and fifty cents; and upon all other such property situated within municipalities, two dollars; and the Legislature shall further provide by general law for increasing the maximum rates authorized to be fixed by the different levying bodies upon all classes of property by submitting the question to the voters of the taxing units affected, but no increase shall be effective unless at least sixty percent of the qualified voters shall favor such increase, and such increase shall not continue for a longer period than three years at any one time, and shall never exceed by more than fifty percent the maximum rate herein provided and prescribed by law . . . but property used for educational, literary, scientific, religious or charitable purposes, all cemeteries, public property, the personal property, including livestock, employed exclusively in agriculture as above defined and the products of agriculture as so defined while owned by the producers may by law be exempted from taxation. . . . The Legislature shall have authority to tax privileges, franchises, and incomes of persons and corporations and to classify and graduate the tax on all incomes according to the amount thereof and to exempt from taxation incomes below a minimum to be fixed from time to time, and such revenues as may be derived from such tax may be appropriated as the Legislature may provide. After the year nineteen hundred thirty-three, the rate of the state tax upon property shall not exceed one cent upon the hundred dollars valuation, except to pay the principal and interest of bonded indebtedness of the State now existing.

Art. X, § 1b. Notwithstanding any other provision of this Constitution to the contrary, the first five thousand dollars of assessed valuation of any real property used exclusively for residential purposes and occupied by the owner or one of the owners thereof as his residence who is a citizen of this State and who is sixty-five years of age or older shall be exempt from ad valorem property taxation, subject to such requirements, limitations and conditions as shall be prescribed by general law.

Art. X, § 6a. . . . (2) the Legislature may impose a state tax or taxes or dedicate a state tax or taxes or any portion thereof for the benefit of and use by counties, municipalities or other political subdivisions of the State for public purposes, the proceeds of any such imposed or dedicated tax or taxes or portion thereof to be distributed to such counties, municipalities or other political subdivisions of the State under such circumstances and subject to such terms, conditions and restrictions as the Legislature may prescribe by law.

Art. X, § 7. County authorities shall never assess taxes, in any one year, the aggregate of which shall exceed ninety-five cents per one hundred dollars' valuation, except for the support of free schools; . . . [payment of indebtedness].

Art. X, § 9. The Legislature may, by law, authorize the corporate authorities of cities, towns and villages, for corporate purposes, to assess and collect taxes; but such taxes shall be uniform, with respect to persons and property within the jurisdiction of the authority imposing the same.

Wisconsin Constitution (1848)

Art. II, § 2. . . . it is hereby ordained that this state shall never interfere with the primary disposal of the soil within the same by the United States . . . and in no case shall nonresident proprietors be taxed higher than residents. . . .

Art. IV, § 31. The legislature is prohibited from enacting any special or private laws in the following cases:

. . . .

   6th. For assessment or collection of taxes or for extending the time for the collection thereof.

. . . .

Art. VIII, § 1. The rule of taxation shall be uniform but the legislature may empower cities, villages or towns to collect and return taxes on real estate located therein by optional methods. Taxes shall be levied upon such property with such classifications as to forests and minerals including or separate or severed from the land, as the legislature shall prescribe. Taxation of agricultural land and undeveloped land, both as defined by law, need not be uniform with the taxation of each other nor with the taxation of other real property. . . . Taxes may also be imposed on incomes, privileges and occupations, which taxes may be graduated and progressive, and reasonable exemptions may be provided.

Wyoming Constitution (1890)

Art. I, § 28. Taxation—Consent of people; uniformity and equality.—No tax shall be imposed without the consent of the people or their authorized representatives. All taxation shall be equal and uniform.

Art. III, § 27. The legislature shall not pass local or special laws in any of the following enumerated cases, that is to say: ... for the assessment or collection of taxes ... extending the time for the collection of taxes ... exempting property from taxation. ...

Art. III, § 37. The legislature shall not delegate to any special commissioner, private corporation or association, any power ... to levy taxes. ...

Art. XIII, § 3. The legislature shall restrict the powers of [municipal] corporations to levy taxes and assessments, to borrow money and contract debts so as to prevent the abuse of such power, and no tax or assessment shall be levied or collected or debts contracted by municipal corporations except in pursuance of law for public purposes specified by law.

Art. XV, § 1. Assessment of lands and improvements thereon.—All lands and improvements thereon shall be listed for assessment, valued for taxation and assessed separately.

Art. XV, § 2. Assessment of coal lands.—All coal lands in the state from which coal is not being mined shall be listed for assessment, valued for taxation and assessed according to value.

Art. XV, § 3. Taxation of mines and mining claims.—All mines and mining claims from which gold, silver and other precious metals, soda, saline, coal, mineral oil or other valuable deposit, is or may be produced shall be taxed in addition to the surface improvements, and in lieu of taxes on the lands, on the gross product thereof, as may be prescribed by law; provided, that the produce of all mines shall be taxed in proportion of the value thereof.

Art. XV, § 4. State levy limited.—For state revenue, there shall be levied annually a tax not to exceed four mills on the dollar of the assessed valuation of the property in the state except for the support of state educational and charitable institutions, the payment of the state debt and the interest thereon.

Art. XV, § 5. County levies limited.—For county revenue, there shall be levied annually a tax not to exceed twelve mills on the dollar for all purposes including general school tax, exclusive of state revenue, except for the payment of its public debt and the interest thereon.

Art. XV, § 11. Uniformity of assessment required.—All property, except as in this constitution otherwise provided, shall be uniformly assessed for taxation, and the legislature shall prescribe such regulations as shall secure a just valuation for taxation of all property, real and personal

Art. XV, § 12. Exemptions from taxation.—The property of the United States, the state, counties, cities, towns, school districts and municipal corporations, when used primarily for a governmental purpose, and public libraries, lot with the buildings thereon used exclusively for religious worship, church parsonages, church schools and public cemeteries, shall be exempt from taxation, and such other property as the legislature may by general law provide.

Art. XV, § 13. Tax must be authorized by law; law to state object.—No tax shall be levied, except in pursuance of law, and every law imposing a tax shall state distinctly the object of the same, to which only it shall be applied.

Art. XV, § 14. Surrender of taxing power prohibited.—The power of taxation shall never be surrendered or suspended by any grant or contract to which the state or any county or other municipal corporation shall be a party.

. . .

Art. XV, § 18. No tax shall be imposed upon income without allowing full credit against such tax liability for all sales, use, and ad valorem taxes paid in the taxable year by the same taxpayer to any taxing authority in Wyoming.

Art. XV, § 19. The Legislature shall provide by law for an excise tax on the privilege of severing or extracting minerals, of one and one-half percent (1½%) on the value of the gross product extracted. The mineral subject to such excise tax shall be coal, petroleum, natural gas, oil shale, and such other minerals as may be designated by the Legislature. Such tax shall be in addition to any other excise, severance or ad valorem tax. The proceeds from such tax shall be deposited in the Permanent Wyoming Mineral Trust Fund, which fund shall remain inviolate. . . .

Art. XXI, § 26. . . . lands belonging to the citizens of the United States residing without this state shall never be taxed at a higher rate than the lands belonging to residents of this state; . . . no taxes shall be imposed by this state on lands or property therein, belonging to, or which may hereafter be purchased by the United States, or reserved for its use. . . .

Tables of Additional Citations

Due Process and Equal Protection Clauses in State Constitutions

	Due Process	Equal Protection
Alabama	Art. I, § 6	
Alaska	Art. I, § 7	Art. I, § 1
Arizona	Art. II, § 4	Art. II, § 13
Arkansas	Art. II, § 8	
California	Art. I, § 7	Id.
Colorado	Art. II, § 25	
Connecticut	Art. I, § 8	Art. I, § 20
Florida	Art. I, § 9	
Georgia	Art. I, § I, para. I	Art. III, § VIII, para. III[a]
Hawaii	Art. I, § 5	Id.
Idaho	Art. I, § 13	
Illinois	Art. I, § 2	Id.
Indiana		Art. I, § 23[b]
Iowa	Art. I, § 9	Art. I, § 6[b]
Kansas	B.Rts. § 18[c]	B.Rts. § 2[b]
Kentucky		B.Rts. § 3[b]
Louisiana	Art. I, § 2	Art. I, § 3
Maine	Art. I, § 6A	Id.
Maryland	D.Rts. art. 23[d]	
Michigan	D.Rts. Art. I, § 17	Art. I, § 2
Minnesota	Art. I, § 7	
Mississippi	Art. III, § 14	
Missouri	Art. I, § 10	
Montana	Art. II, § 17	
Nebraska	Art. I, § 3	
Nevada	Art. 1, § 8	
New Hampshire		Pt. I, art. 2[b]
New Mexico	Art. II, § 18	Id.
New York	Art. I, § 6	Art. I, § 11
North Carolina	Art. I, § 19[d]	Id.
North Dakota	Art. I, § 13	
Oklahoma	Art. II, § 7	
Ohio		Art. II, § 26[b]
Oregon		Art. I, § 20[b]
(Puerto Rico)	Art. II, § 7	Id.
South Carolina	Art. I, § 3	Id.
South Dakota	Art. VI, § 2	Art. VI, § 18
Texas	Art. I, § 19[c]	Art. I, § 3[b]
Utah	Art. I, § 7	
Virginia	Art. I, § 11	
Washington	Art. I, § 3	
West Virginia	Art. III, § 10	
Wyoming	Art. I, § 6	

[a]The Georgia Constitution contains a provision dealing with equal protection which may have special significance for regulatory measures: "The exercise of the police power of the state shall never be abridged, nor so construed as to permit the conduct of business in such manner as to infringe the equal rights of others, or the general well-being of the state." See also: art. I, & II, para. III.

[b]There is some overlapping with clauses prohibiting special privileges and immunities, e.g., Indiana provides: "The General Assembly shall not grant to any citizen, or class of

citizens, privileges or immunities, which, upon the same terms shall not equally belong to all citizens." Other types of provisions overlap with general uniformity or general equality, e.g., Iowa: "All laws of a general nature shall have uniform operation"; New Hampshire: "Equality of rights under the law shall not be abridged by the state on account of race, creed, color, sex or national origin"; some may be combinations of all of these. See also: Kansas, Kentucky, Ohio, Oregon, Texas and Utah. Refer to the second table for prohibitions against special privileges and immunities.

[c] The wording "due course" is used instead.

[d] The wording "law of the land" may be equivalent. *Cf.*: Del. art. I, § 7; Mass. D.Rts. art. XII; N.H. B.Rts. art. 15; Pa. art. I, § 9; R.I. art. I, § 10; Tenn. art. I, § 8; Vt. art. I, § 10.

Prohibitions Against Special Privileges or Immunities in State Constitutions

Alabama	Art. IV, § 104; art. I, § 22[a]
Alaska	Art. I, § 15[a]
Arizona	Art. II, §§ 9[a] and 13; art. IV, § 19 (13)
Arkansas	Art. II, § 18; art. II, § 3
California	Art. I, § 7 (b)
Colorado	Art. V, § 25; art. II, § 11[a]
Connecticut	Art. I, § 1
Florida	Art. III, § 11 (12)
Georgia	Art. I, § I, para. VII[a]
Hawaii	Art. I, § 21[a]
Idaho	Art. I, § 2[a]
Indiana	Art. I, § 23
Iowa	Art. VIII, § 12; art. I, § 6
Kansas	B.Rts. § 2
Kentucky	B.Rts. § 3
Louisiana	Art. III, § 12 (7); art. XII, § 12
Minnesota	Art. XII, § 1
Missouri	Art. III, § 40 (28); art. I, § 13[a]
Montana	Art. II, § 31[a]
Nebraska	Art. III, § 18; art. I, § 16[a]
New Hampshire	Pt. I, art. 10
New Jersey	Art. IV, § VII, 9 (8)
New Mexico	Art. IV, § 24
New York	Art. III, §§ 17 and 21
North Carolina	Art. I, § 32
North Dakota	Art. I, § 20[a]; art. II, § 69 (20)
Ohio	Art. I, § 2[a]
Oklahoma	Art. V, § 51
Oregon	Art. I, § 20
Pennsylvania	Art. I, § 17[a]
(Puerto Rico)	Art. VI, § 13[a]
South Dakota	Art. VI, §§ 12[a] and 18; art. III, § 23
Tennessee	Art. XI, § 8
Texas	Art. I, § 3; art. I, § 17[a]
Utah	Art. I, § 23[a]
Vermont	Ch. I, art. 7
Virginia	Art. I, § 4; art. IV, § 14 (18)
Washington	Art. I, §§ 8[a] and 12
Wyoming	Art. I, § 3; art. III, § 27

[a] Prohibition relates to aspects of irrevocability.

Prohibitions against Excessive Fines in State Constitutions

Alabama	Art. I, § 15
Alaska	Art. I, § 12
Arizona	Art. II, § 15
Arkansas	Art. II, § 9
California	Art. I, § 17
Colorado	Art. II, § 20
Connecticut	Art. I, § 8
Delaware	Art. I, § 11
Florida	Art. I, § 17
Georgia	Art. I, § I, para. XIV.
Hawaii	Art. I, § 12
Idaho	Art. I, § 6
Indiana	Art. I, § 16
Iowa	Art. I, § 17
Kansas	B.Rts. § 9
Kentucky	B.Rts. § 17
Maine	Art. I, § 9
Maryland	D.Rts. art. 25
Massachusetts	D.Rts. Pt. I, art. 26
Michigan	D.Rts. art. I, § 16
Minnesota	Art. I, § 5
Mississippi	Art. III, § 28
Missouri	Art. I, § 21
Montana	Art. I, § 22
Nebraska	Art. I, § 9
Nevada	Art. 1, § 6
New Hampshire	Pt. I, art. 33
New Jersey	Art. I, § 12
New Mexico	Art. II, § 13
New York	Art. I, § 5
North Carolina	Art. I, § 27
North Dakota	Art. I, § 6
Ohio	Art. I, § 9
Oklahoma	Art. II, § 9
Oregon	Art. I, § 16
Pennsylvania	Art. I, § 13
(Puerto Rico)	Art. II, § 11
Rhode Island	Art. I, § 8
South Carolina	Art. I, § 15
South Dakota	Art. VI, § 23
Tennessee	Art. I, § 16
Texas	Art. I, § 13
Utah	Art. I, § 9
Virginia	Art. I, § 9
Washington	Art. I, § 14
West Virginia	Art. III, § 5
Wisconsin	Art. I, § 6
Wyoming	Art. I, § 14

Separation of Powers Requirements in State Constitutions

Alabama	Art. III, §§ 42 and 43
Arizona	Art. III
Arkansas	Art. IV, §§ 1 and 2
California	Art. III, § 3
Colorado	Art. III
Connecticut	Art. II
Florida	Art. II, § 3
Georgia	Art. I, § II, para. IV
Idaho	Art. II, § 1
Illinois	Art. II, § 1
Indiana	Art. III, § 1
Iowa	Art. III, § 1
Kentucky	§§ 27 and 28
Louisiana	Art. II, §§ 1 and 2
Maine	Art. III, §§ 1 and 2
Maryland	D.Rts. art. 8
Massachusetts	D.Rts. Pt. I, art. 30
Michigan	Art. III, § 2
Minnesota	Art. III, § 1
Mississippi	Art. I, §§ 1 and 2
Missouri	Art. II, § 1
Montana	Art. III, § 1
Nebraska	Art. II, § 1
Nevada	Art. 3, § 1
New Hampshire	Pt. I, § 37
New Jersey	Art. III
New Mexico	Art. III, § 1
North Carolina	Art. I, § 6
Oklahoma	Art. IV, § 1
Oregon	Art. III, § 1
Rhode Island	Art. III
South Carolina	Art. I, § 8
South Dakota	Art. II
Tennessee	Art. II, §§ 1 and 2
Texas	Art. II, § 1
Utah	Art. V, § 1
Vermont	Ch. II, § 5
Virginia	Art. I, § 5; art. III, § 1
West Virginia	Art. V, § 1
Wyoming	Art. II, § 1

Municipal Charters and Home Rule Provisions in State Constitutions

Alaska	Art. X, § 11
Arizona	Art. XIII, § 2
Arkansas	Art. XII
California	Art. XI
Colorado	Art. XX, §§ 4, 5, 6
Connecticut	Art. X
Florida	Art. VIII
Georgia	Art. IX
Hawaii	Art. VIII
Illinois	Art. VII, § 6
Iowa	Amend. 2 of 1968; amend. of 1978 to art. III
Kansas	Art. 12, § 5
Louisiana	Art. VI, §§ 4, 5, 6, 8
Maine	Art. VIII, pt. II
Maryland	Art. XI-A, -E, -F
Massachusetts	Art. LXXXIX, arts. of amend.
Michigan	Art. VII, §§ 2, 22
Minnesota	Art. XII
Missouri	Art. VI, §§ 18 (a)-(l), 19-22, 30 (a)
Montana	Art. XI, §§ 5, 6
Nebraska	Art. XI
Nevada	Art. 8, § 8
New Hampshire	Pt. I, art. 39
New Mexico	Art. X, §§ 4, 5
New York	Art. IX
North Dakota	Art. VI
Ohio	Art. XVIII, §§ 3, 7; art. X
Oklahoma	Art. XVIII, §§ 3(a)
Oregon	Art. VI, § 10; art. XI, § 2
Pennsylvania	Art. III, § 32; art. IX
Rhode Island	Art. XXVIII of amends.
South Carolina	Art. VIII, § 11
South Dakota	Art. IX, § 2
Tennessee	Art. XI, § 9
Texas	Art. XI, § 4, 5
Utah	Art. XI, § 5
Virginia	Art. VII, §§ 2, 3
Washington	Art. XI, §§ 4, 10, 16
West Virginia	Art. VI, § 39 (a)
Wisconsin	Art. XI, § 3

Appendix A
Summary of Proposition 13 (Jarvis-Gann Initiative) Amendment to Art. XIII A of the California Constitution

Arlo Woolery

Summary of Provisions

1. Limits ad valorem tax on *real property* to 1 percent of full cash value.
2. Does not apply to ad valorem taxes on special assessments to pay interest and redemption charges on debt issued prior to the effective date of the amendment.
3. Defines "full cash value" as
   a. The county assessor's valuation shown on the 1975-76 tax bill.
   b. Or the appraised value of real property when purchased or newly constructed or when a change in ownership has occurred after the 1975 assessment.
4. Allows reassessment of real property up to 1975-1976 tax levels.
5. Allows annual increases of fair market value[a] not to exceed 2 percent or reductions in value based on some economic index.
6. Requires a two-thirds vote of all members elected to each of the two houses of the legislature to increase tax revenues by increasing rates or changing methods of computation.
7. Prohibits any new ad valorem taxes on real property.
8. Prohibits any sales or transaction taxes on real property.
9. Allows cities, counties, and special districts to impose special taxes if approved by a two-thirds vote of the *qualified electors.*

Summary of Immediate Effects on Assessment Administration in California

1. All current assessments of property owned by the present owner since 1975 must be rolled back to 1975 values and the 1975 values may be increased no more than 2 percent annually to obtain current market value.[a]

---
[a] A November 1978 amendment substituted the words "full cash value". See appendix B.

2. Properties that have changed ownership or have been newly constructed since 1975 must be reappraised as of the sale date or the date construction was complete.
3. Assessors must revalue as of 1975 those properties not already at their 1975 full cash value.
4. If a divided partial interest in a property is sold, the part sold must be reappraised at market value as of the sale date.
5. State assessed property (railroads, utilities, etc.) will be rolled back to 1975 values.

**Appendix B
New Constitutional
Amendments (to
Beginning of 1979)**

Alabama Constitution

Amendment No. 373

§ I. (a), (b) All taxable property within this State, not exempt by law, shall be divided and assessed into the following classes for the purpose of ad valorem taxes:

Class I. All property of utilities used in the business of such utilities at 30 per centum.

Class II. All property not otherwise classified at 20 per centum.

Class III. All agricultural, forest and single-family owner-occupied residential property and historic buildings and sites at 10 per centum.

Class IV. All private passenger automobiles and motor pickup trucks personally or privately owned and operated, not for hire, rent or compensation at 15 per centum.

(c) With respect to ad valorem taxes levied by the State and/or counties, municipalities or other authorities all taxable property shall be forever taxed at the same ratio of assessed value to fair market value, except as otherwise provided in this Amendment.

(d) No class of taxable property shall have an assessment ratio of less than 5 per centum or more than 35 per centum.

(e) A taxing authority may decrease any rate at any time, provided the decrease shall not jeopardize the payment of any bonded indebtedness secured by such tax. The tax assessor shall compute and certify to each county authority the amount that will be produced by every levy for the tax year. A taxing authority may increase the rate provided in this Constitution, provided that any such millage increase shall not exceed 20% above the total mills imposed by the taxing authority with respect to such tax on each dollar of taxable property situated in the taxing authority for the preceding tax year.

(f) Any taxing authority may increase the rate provided the proposed increase shall have been (1) proposed by the authority having power to levy tax after a public hearing on such proposal, (2) approved by the Legislature, (3) approved by a majority vote of qualified electors residing in the taxing authority at a special election.

(g) The Legislature is authorized to enact legislation to implement the provisions of this amendment and may provide for exemptions from taxation.

(h) Where any Constitutional provision or statute provides for any taxing authority to levy taxes, borrow money, or incur indebtedness in relation to property assessment therein for State and County taxes, such provision shall mean as assessed for county or municipal taxes as the case may be.

(i) Any provision of the Constitution to the contrary notwithstanding, annual ad valorem taxes with respect to any item of taxable property described as Class I property shall never exceed 2% of the fair and reasonable market value of such taxable property, with respect to any item of Class II property shall never exceed 1½% of the fair and reasonable market value of such taxable property, such amount with respect to any item of Class IV property shall never exceed 1¼% of the fair and reasonable market value of such taxable property, and such amount with respect to any item of Class III property shall never exceed 1% of the fair and reasonable market value of such taxable property.

(j) After October 1, 1978, taxable property defined as Class III property shall, upon application by the owner of such property, be assessed at the ratio of assessed value to the current use value of such taxable property and not the fair and reasonable market value of such property.

(k) The following property shall be exempt from all ad valorem taxation: the real and personal property of the state, counties and municipalities and property devoted exclusively to religious, educational or charitable purposes, household and kitchen furniture, all farm tractors, all farming implements when used exclusively in connection with agricultural property and all stocks of goods, wares and merchandise.

(l) A taxing authority may impose and levy an additional ad valorem tax of not more than two mills on all taxable property in order to reimburse itself for its payment of such costs of reappraisal or to pay any unpaid costs or its pro rata share of such unpaid costs of reappraisal.

(m) If any portion of this section should be declared invalid by any court of competent jurisdiction, such invalidity shall not affect the validity of any of the remaining portions of this section, which shall continue effective.

California Constitution

Art. XIII A, § 2. (a) The full cash value means the [County Assessors] *county assessor's* valuation of real property as shown on the 1975-76 tax bill under "full cash value"; or, thereafter, the appraised value of real property when purchased, newly constructed, or a change in ownership has [occured] *occurred* after the 1975 assessment. All real property not already assessed up to the 1975-76 [tax levels] *full cash value* may be reassessed to reflect that valuation. *For purposes of this section, the term "newly constructed" shall not include real property which is reconstructed after a disaster, as declared by the Governor, where the fair market value of such real property, as reconstructed, is comparable to its fair market value prior to the disaster.*

(b) The [fair market] *full cash* value base may reflect from year to year the inflationary rate not to exceed [two] *2* percent [2%] for any given year or reduction as shown in the consumer price index or comparable data for the area under taxing jurisdiction [.] , *or may be reduced to reflect substantial damage, destruction or other factors causing a decline in value.*

Italicized provisions are those that have been newly added to the existing text. Those shown in brackets [ ] are to be deleted from the text.

Hawaii Constitution

Art. VIII, § 3.[a] The taxing power shall be reserved to the State, except so much thereof as may be delegated by the legislature to the political subdivisions, and [the] *except that all functions, powers and duties relating to the taxation of real property shall be exercised exclusively by the counties, with the exception of the county of Kalawao.* The legislature shall have the power to apportion state revenues among the several political subdivisions.

Art. XVIII, § 6. *The amendment to Section 3 of Article VIII shall take effect on the first day of July after two full calendar years have elapsed following the ratification of such amendment; provided that for a period of eleven years following such ratification, the policies and methods of assessing real property taxes shall be uniform throughout the State and shall be established by agreement of a majority of the political subdivisions. Each political subdivision shall enact such uniform policies and methods of assessment by ordinance before the effective date of this amendment, and in the event the political subdivisions fail to enact such ordinances, the uniform policies and methods of assessment shall be established by general law. Any amendments to the uniform policies and methods of assessment established by the political subdivisions may only be made by agreement of a majority of the political subdivisions and enactment thereof by ordinance in each political subdivision.*

Real property tax exemptions and dedications of land for specific use for assessment at its value in such use as provided by law and in effect upon ratification of the amendment to Section 3 of Article VIII shall be enacted by ordinance and shall not be eliminated or diminished for a period of eleven years following such ratification; provided that increases in such exemptions, or the additions of new and further exemptions or dedications of lands, may be established or granted only by agreement of a majority of the political subdivisions, and such increases or additions shall be enacted by ordinance in each political subdivision.

Italicized provisions are those that have been newly added to the existing text. Those shown in brackets thus [ ] are to be deleted from the text.

The effective date under the terms of the schedule of art. XVIII, § 6 would be July 1, 1981.

[a] Art. VIII was previously numbered art. VII.

Louisiana Constitution

Art. IX, § 9. First Use Tax Trust Fund.

(A) (1) **Creation.** The First Use Tax Trust Fund is hereby created and established in the state treasury as a special and irrevocable trust fund for the deposit of the proceeds, and interest derived therefrom, of the first use tax imposed by law in 1978 or thereafter and any other tax imposed by law which would have the effect of imposing any new or alternative tax on uses of those resources subject to the tax levied by the first use tax. . . .[a]

(A) (3) (A) **Barrier Islands Conservation Account.** Twenty-five percent of the proceeds of the tax shall be maintained in an account in the First Use Tax Trust Fund to be known as the "Barrier Islands Conservation Account". . . .

---

[a] This is intended to relate to natural gas.

Maine Constitution

Art. IV, Pt. 3, § 23. Municipalities reimbursed annually. The Legislature shall annually reimburse each municipality from state tax sources for 50% of the property tax revenue loss suffered by that municipality during the previous calendar year because of statutory property tax exemptions or credits enacted after April 1, 1978. The Legislature shall enact appropriate legislation to carry out the intent of this section.

Art. IX, § 8. Taxation; intangible property; permits valuation of certain lands upon current use; proviso; school districts. All taxes upon real and personal estate, assessed by authority of this State, shall be apportioned and assessed equally according to the just value thereof.

    1. The Legislature shall have power to levy a tax upon intangible personal property at such rate as it deems wise and equitable without regard to the rate applied to other classes of property.

    2. The Legislature shall have power to provide for the assessment of the following types of real estate whenever [*sic*] situated in accordance with a valuation based upon the current use thereof and in accordance with such conditions as the Legislature may enact:

        A. Farms and agricultural lands, timberlands and woodlands;

        B. Open space lands which are used for recreation or the enjoyment of scenic [a] natural beauty; and

        C. Lands used for game management or wildlife sanctuaries.

    In implementing paragraphs A, B and C, the Legislature shall provide that any change of use higher than those set forth in paragraphs A, B and C, except when the change is occasioned by a transfer resulting from the exercise or threatened exercise of the power of eminent domain, shall result in the imposition of a minimum penalty equal to the tax which would have been imposed over the 5 years preceding that change of use had that real estate been assessed at its highest and best use, less all taxes paid on that real estate over the preceding 5 years, and interest, upon such reasonable and equitable basis as the Legislature shall determine.

    3. The Legislature shall have power to provide that taxes, which it may authorize a School Administrative District or a community school district to levy, may be assessed on real, personal and intangible property in accordance with any cost-sharing formula which it may authorize.

---

[a] The word "or" was probably dropped inadvertently from the previous reading of the text.

Massachusetts Constitution

Article IV of chapter 1 of Part the Second of the Constitution is hereby amended by inserting after the words "and to impose and levy proportional and reasonable assessments, rates and taxes, upon all the inhabitants of, and persons resident, and estates lying, within said Commonwealth" the words:—, except that, in addition to the powers conferred under Articles XLI and XCIX of the Amendments, the general court may classify real property according to its use in no more than four classes and to assess, rate and tax such property differently in the classes so established, but proportionately in the same class, and except that reasonable exemptions may be granted.

Article XLI of the Amendments to the Constitution is hereby annulled and the following Article is adopted in place thereof:—

Full power and authority are hereby given and granted to the general court to prescribe for wild or forest lands and lands retained in a natural state for the preservation of wildlife and other natural resources and lands for recreational uses, such methods of taxation as will develop and conserve the forest resources, wildlife and other natural resources and the environmental benefits of recreational lands within the commonwealth.

Michigan Constitution

Art. IX, § 25. Property taxes and other local taxes and state taxation and spending may not be increased above the limitations specified herein without direct voter approval. The state is prohibited from requiring any new or expanded activities by local governments without full state financing, from reducing the proportion of state spending in the form of aid to local governments, or from shifting the tax burden to local government. A provision for emergency conditions is established and the repayment of voter approved bonded indebtedness is guaranteed. Implementation of this section is specified in Sections 26 through 34, inclusive, of this Article.

Art. IX, § 26. There is hereby established a limit on the total amount of taxes which may be imposed by the legislature in any fiscal year on the taxpayers of this state. This limit shall not be changed without approval of the majority of the qualified electors voting thereon, as provided for in Article 12 of the Constitution. Effective with fiscal year 1979-1980, and for each fiscal year thereafter, the legislature shall not impose taxes of any kind which, together with all other revenues of the state, federal aid excluded, exceed the revenue limit established in this section. The revenue limit shall be equal to the product of the ratio of Total State Revenues in fiscal year 1978-1979 divided by the Personal Income of Michigan in calendar year 1977 multiplied by the Personal Income of Michigan in either the prior calendar year or the average of Personal Income of Michigan in the previous three calendar years, whichever is greater.

For any fiscal year in the event that Total State Revenues exceed the revenue limit established in this section by 1% or more, the excess revenues shall be refunded pro rata based on the liability reported on the Michigan income tax and single business tax (or its successor tax or taxes) annual returns filed following the close of such fiscal year. If the excess is less than 1%, this excess may be transferred to the State Budget Stabilization Fund.

The revenue limitation established in this section shall not apply to taxes imposed for the payment of principal and interest on bonds, approved by the voters and authorized under Section 15 of this Article, and loans to school districts authorized under Section 16 of this Article.

If responsibility for funding a program or programs is transferred from one level of government to another, as a consequence of constitutional amendment, the state revenue and spending limits may be adjusted to accommodate such change, provided that the total revenue authorized for collection by both state and local governments does not exceed that amount which would have been authorized without such change.

Art. IX, § 27. The revenue limit of Section 26 of this Article may be exceeded only if all of the following conditions are met: (1) The governor requests the legislature to declare an emergency; (2) the request is specific as to the nature of the emergency, the dollar amount of the emergency, and the method by which the emergency will be funded; and (3) the legislature thereafter declares an emergency in accordance with the specifics of the governor's request by a two-thirds vote of the members elected to and serving in each house. The emergency must be declared in accordance with this section prior to incurring any of the expenses which constitute the emergency request. The revenue limit may be exceeded only during the fiscal year for which the emergency is declared. In no event shall any part of the amount representing a refund under Section 26 of this Article be the subject of an emergency request.

Art. IX, § 28. No expenses of state government shall be incurred in any fiscal year which exceed the sum of the revenue limit established in Sections 26 and 27 of this Article plus federal aid and any surplus from a previous fiscal year.

Art. IX, § 29. The state is hereby prohibited from reducing the state financed proportion of the necessary costs of any existing activity or service required of units of Local Government by state law. A new activity or service or an increase in the level of any activity or service beyond that required by existing law shall not be required by the legislature or any state agency of units of Local Government, unless a state appropriation is made and disbursed to pay the unit of Local Government for any necessary increased costs. The provision of this section shall not apply to costs incurred pursuant to Article VI, Section 18.

Art. IX, § 30. The proportion of total state spending paid to all units of Local Government, taken as a group, shall not be reduced below that proportion in effect in fiscal year 1978-79.

Art. IX, § 31. Units of Local Government are hereby prohibited from levying any tax not authorized by law or charter when this section is ratified or from increasing the rate of an existing tax above that rate authorized by law or charter when this section is ratified, without the approval of a majority of the qualified electors of that unit of Local Government voting thereon. If the definition of the base of an existing tax is broadened, the maximum authorized rate of taxation on the new base in each unit of Local Government shall be reduced to yield the same estimated gross revenue as on the prior base. If the assessed valuation of property as finally equalized, excluding the value of new construction and improvements, increases by a larger percentage than the increase in the General Price Level from the previous year, the maximum authorized rate applied thereto in each unit of Local Government shall be reduced to yield the same gross revenue from existing property, adjusted for changes in the General Price Level, as could have been collected at the existing authorized rate on the prior assessed value.

The limitations of this section shall not apply to taxes imposed for the payment of principal and interest on bonds or other evidence of indebtedness or for the payment of assessments on contract obligations in anticipation of which bonds are issued which were authorized prior to the effective date of this amendment.

Art. IX, § 32. Any taxpayer of the state shall have standing to bring suit in the Michigan State Court of Appeals to enforce the provisions of Sections 25 through 31, inclusive, of this Article and, if the suit is sustained, shall receive from the applicable unit of government his costs incurred in maintaining such suit.

Art. IX, § 33. Definitions. The definitions of this section shall apply to Section 25 through 32 of Article IX, inclusive.

"Total State Revenues" includes all general and special revenues, excluding federal aid, as defined in the budget message of the governor for fiscal year 1978-1979. Total State Revenues shall exclude the amount of any credits based on actual tax liabilities or the imputed tax components of rental payments, but shall include the amount of any credits not related to actual tax liabilities. "Personal Income of Michigan" is the total income received by persons in Michigan from all sources, as defined and officially reported by the United States Department of Commerce or its successor agency. "Local Government" means any political subdivision of the state, including, but not restricted to, school districts, cities, villages, townships, charter townships, counties, charter counties, authorities created by the state, and authorities created by other units of local government. "General Price Level" means the Consumer Price Index for the United States as defined and officially reported by the United States Department of Labor or its successor agency.

Art. IX, § 34. The Legislature shall implement the provisions of Sections 25 through 33, inclusive, of this Article.

Missouri Constitution

Art. X, § 10(c). The general assembly may require by law that political subdivisions reduce the rate of levy of all property taxes the subdivisions impose whether the rate of levy is authorized by this constitution or by law. The general assembly may by law establish the method of increasing reduced rates of levy in subsequent years.

Art. X, § 12(a). In addition to the rates authorized in section 11 for county purposes, the county court in the several counties not under township organization, the township board of directors in the counties under township organization, and the proper administrative body in counties adopting an alternative form of government, may levy an additional tax, not exceeding fifty cents on each hundred dollars assessed valuation, all of such tax to be collected and turned in to the county treasury to be used for road and bridge purposes; provided that, before any such county may increase its tax levy for road and bridge purposes above thirty-five cents it must submit such increase to the qualified voters of that county at a general or special election and receive the approval of a majority of the voters voting on such increase. In addition to the above levy for road and bridge purposes, it shall be the duty of the county court, when so authorized by a majority of the qualified electors of any road district, general or special, voting thereon at an election held for such purpose, to make an additional levy of not to exceed thirty-five cents on the hundred dollars assessed valuation on all taxable real and tangible personal property within such district, to be collected in the same manner as state and county taxes, and placed to the credit of the road district authorizing such levy, such election to be called and held in the manner provided by law provided that the general assembly may require by law that the rates authorized herein may be reduced.

Nebraska Constitution

Amendment to Art. VIII, § 1. The necessary revenue of the state and its governmental subdivisions shall be raised by taxation in such manner as the Legislature may direct. Taxes shall be levied by valuation uniformly and proportionately upon all tangible property and franchises, except *(1)* that the Legislature may provide for a different method of taxing motor vehicles and may also establish a separate class of motor vehicles consisting of those owned and held for resale by motor vehicle dealers which shall be taxed in the manner and to the extent as provided by the Legislature and may also establish a separate class for trucks, trailers, semi-trailers, truck-tractors, or combinations thereof, consisting of those owned by residents and nonresidents of this state, and operating in interstate commerce, and may provide reciprocal and proportionate taxation of such vehicles; *Provided*, that such tax proceeds from motor vehicles taxed in each county shall be allocated to the state, counties, townships, cities, villages, and school districts of such county in the same proportion that the levy of each bears to the total levy of said county on [personal tangible] *real* property *and (2) when a political subdivision authorized to levy a tax or cause a tax to be levied lies in two or more counties, and one or more of such counties have not completed a general reappraisal of all land and improvements within two years of one another, the State Board of Equalization and Assessment shall fix separate and distinct tax levies so that the county which has most recently completed a general reappraisal of all lands and improvements shall provide the same percentage of the political subdivision's budget as it provided prior to such reappraisal. For all tax years commencing on or after January 1, 1981, the State Board of Equalization and Assessment shall not be empowered to fix separate and distinct levies but shall annually review and equalize assessments of property among counties.* The Legislature may enact laws to provide that the value of land actively devoted to agricultural or horticultural use shall, for property tax purposes, be that value which such land has for agricultural or horticultural use without regard to any value which such land might have for other purposes or uses, and prescribe standards and methods for the determination of the value of real or other tangible property at uniform and proportionate values. Taxes uniform as to class of property or the ownership or use thereof may be levied by valuation or otherwise upon classes of intangible property as the Legislature may determine, and such intangible property held in trust or otherwise for the purpose of funding pension,

---

The words shown in brackets thus [ ] are to be deleted from the text. Words that have been italicized are new additions to the text of art. VIII, § 1.

profit-sharing, or other employee benefit plans as defined by the Legislature may be declared to be exempt from taxation. Taxes, other than property taxes, may be authorized by law. Existing revenue laws shall continue in effect until changed by the Legislature. The Legislature may provide that livestock shall constitute a separate and distinct class of property for purposes of taxation and may further provide for reciprocal and proportionate taxation of livestock located in this state for only part of a year.

South Dakota Constitution

Art. XI. (New Section).

The rate of taxation imposed by the state of South Dakota on personal or corporate income or on sales or services, or the allowable levies or the percentage basis for determining valuation as fixed by law for purposes of taxation on real or personal property, shall not be increased unless by the consent of the people by exercise of their right of initiative or by two-thirds vote of all the members elect of each branch of the Legislature.

Texas Constitution

Art. VIII, § 1. Taxation shall be equal and Uniform.

All *real property and tangible personal* property in this State, whether owned by natural persons or corporations, other than municipal, shall be taxed in proportion to its value, which shall be ascertained as may be provided by law. The Legislature may *provide for the taxation of intangible property and* [impose a poll tax. It] may also impose occupation taxes, both upon natural persons and upon corporations, other than municipal, doing any business in this State. It may also tax incomes of both natural persons and corporations other than municipal, except that persons engaged in mechanical and agricultural pursuits shall never be required to pay an occupation tax. *The Legislature by general law shall exempt* [; Provided, that two hundred and fifty dollars worth of] household *goods not held or used for the production of income and personal effects not held or used for the production of income, and the Legislature by general law may exempt all or part of the personal property homestead of a family or single adult, "personal property homestead" meaning that personal property exempt by law from forced sale for debt,* [and kitchen furniture, belonging to each family in this State shall be exempt] from *ad valorem* taxation. *The* [, and provided further that the] occupation tax levied by any county, city or town for any year on persons or corporations pursuing any profession or business, shall not exceed one half of the tax levied by the State for the same period on such profession or business.

Art. VIII, § 1-b. (b) From and after January 1, 1973, the governing body of any county, city, town, school district, or other political subdivision of the State may exempt by its own action not less than Three Thousand Dollars ($3,000) of the *market* [assessed] value of residence homesteads *of persons, married or unmarried, including those living alone, who are under a disability for purposes of payment of disability insurance benefits under Federal Old-Age, Survivors, and Disability Insurance or its successor or* of married or unmarried persons sixty-five (65) years of age or older, including those living alone, from all ad valorem taxes thereafter levied by the political subdivision. As an alternative, upon receipt of a petition signed by twenty percent (20%) of the voters who voted in the last preceding election held by the political subdivision, the governing body of the subdivision shall call an election to determine by majority vote whether an amount not less than Three Thousand Dollars ($3,000) as provided in the petition, of the *market* [assessed] value of residence homesteads *of disabled persons or* of persons sixty-five (65) years of age or over shall be exempt from

---

These provisions took effect January 1, 1979.

Italicized provisions are those that have been newly added to the existing text. Those shown in brackets thus [ ] are to be deleted from the text.

ad valorem taxes thereafter levied by the political subdivision. *An eligible disabled person who is sixty-five (65) years of age or older may not receive both exemptions from the same political subdivision in the same year but may choose either if the subdivision has adopted both.* Where any ad valorem tax has theretofore been pledged for the payment of any debt, the taxing officers of the political subdivision shall have authority to continue to levy and collect the tax against the homestead property at the same rate as the tax so pledged until the debt is discharged, if the cessation of the levy would impair the obligation of the contract by which the debt was created. *An exemption adopted under this subsection based on assessed value is increased, effective January 1, 1979, to an amount that, when converted to market value, provides the same reduction in taxes, except that the market value exemption shall be rounded to the nearest $100.*

Art. VIII, § 1-b. *(c) Five Thousand Dollars ($5,000) of the market value of the residence homestead of a married or unmarried adult, including one living alone, is exempt from ad valorem taxation for general elementary and secondary public school purposes. In addition to this exemption, the legislature by general law may exempt an amount not to exceed Ten Thousand ($10,000) of the market value of the residence homestead of a person who is disabled as defined in Subsection (b) of this section and of a person sixty-five (65) years of age or older from ad valorem taxation for general elementary and secondary school purposes. The legislature by general law may base the amount of and condition eligibility for the additional exemption authorized by this subsection for disabled persons and for persons sixty-five (65) years of age or older on economic need. An eligible disabled person who is sixty-five (65) years of age or older may not receive both exemptions from a school district but may choose either. An eligible person is entitled to receive both the exemption required by this subsection for all residence homesteads and any exemption adopted pursuant to Subsection (b) of this section, but the legislature shall provide by general law whether an eligible disabled or elderly person may receive both the additional exemption for the elderly and disabled authorized by this subsection and any exemption for the elderly or disabled adopted pursuant to Subsection (b) of this section. Where ad valorem tax has previously been pledged for the payment of debt, the taxing officers of a school district may continue to levy and collect the tax against the value of homesteads exempted under this subsection until the debt is discharged if the cessation of the levy would impair the obligation of the contract by which the debt was created. The legislature shall provide for formulas to protect school districts against all or part of the revenue loss incurred by the implementation of Article VIII, Sections 1-b(c), 1-b(d), and 1-d-1, of this constitution. The legislature by general law may define residence homestead for purposes of this section.*

Art. VIII, § 1-b. *(d) Except as otherwise provided by this subsection, if a person* receives the residence homestead exemption prescribed by Subsection (c) of this section for homesteads of persons sixty-five (65) years of age or older, the total amount of ad valorem taxes imposed on that homestead for general elementary and secondary public school purposes may not be increased while it remains the residence homestead of that person or that person's spouse who receives the exemption. However, those taxes may be increased to the extent the value of the homestead is increased by improvements other than repairs or improvements made to comply with governmental requirements.

Art. VIII, § 1-d-1. *(a)* To promote the preservation of open-space land, the legislature shall provide by general law for taxation of open-space land devoted to farm or ranch purposes on the basis of its productive capacity and may provide by general law for taxation of open-space land devoted to timber production on the basis of its productive capacity. The legislature by general law may provide eligibility limitations under this section and may impose sanctions in furtherance of the taxation policy of this section.

(b) If a property owner qualifies his land for designation for agricultural use under Section 1-d of this article, the land is subject to the provisions of Section 1-d for the year in which the designation is effective and is not subject to a law enacted under this Section 1-d-1 in that year.

Art. VIII, § 21. *(a)* Subject to any exceptions prescribed by general law, the total amount of property taxes imposed by a political subdivision in any year may not exceed the total amount of property taxes imposed by that subdivision in the preceding year unless the governing body of the subdivision gives notice of its intent to consider an increase in taxes and holds a public hearing on the proposed increase before it increases those total taxes. The legislature shall prescribe by law the form, content, timing, and methods of giving the notice and the rules for the conduct of the hearing.

(b) In calculating the total amount of taxes imposed in the current year for the purposes of Subsection (a) of this section, the taxes on property in territory added to the political subdivision since the preceding year and on new improvements that were not taxable in the preceding year are excluded. In calculating the total amount of taxes imposed in the preceding year for the purposes of subsection (a) of this section, the taxes imposed on real property that is not taxable by the subdivision in the current year are excluded.

(c) The legislature by general law shall require that, subject to reasonable exceptions, a property owner be given notice of a revaluation and of the amount of taxes that will result from the reappraised value if neither the tax rate nor the ratio of assessment in effect in the preceding year is reduced. The notice must be given before the procedures required in Subsection (a) are instituted.

Art. VIII, § 23. *(a)* There shall be no statewide appraisal of real property for ad valorem tax purposes; however, this shall not preclude formula distribution of tax revenues to political subdivisions of the state.

(b) Administrative and judicial enforcement of uniform standards and procedures for appraisal of property for ad valorem tax purposes, as prescribed by general law, shall originate in the county where the tax is imposed, except that the legislature may provide by general law for political subdivisions with boundaries extending outside the county.

Virginia Constitution

Art. X, § 6. (h) The General Assembly may by general law authorize the governing body of any county, city, town, or regional government to provide for a partial exemption from local real property taxation, within such restrictions and upon such conditions as may be prescribed, of real estate whose improvements, by virtue of age and use, have undergone substantial renovation, rehabilitation or replacement.

About the Author

Michael M. Bernard is a Fellow at the Lincoln Institute of Land Policy in Cambridge, Massachusetts, where he is doing work in law, taxation, and land use controls. He received the A.B. degree from the University of Chicago and J.D. from Northwestern University School of Law. After being admitted to the bar in Illinois and New York, he obtained a master's degree in planning from Harvard University. He has written, taught, and consulted in the areas of public policy analysis and legal reform for a number of years. He served as a planning consultant and attorney-advisor in Puerto Rico, as planning and legal advisor to the city of Chicago, and as a consultant to Arthur D. Little, Inc. and the White House Policy Advisory Committee to the District Commissioners in an evaluation of District of Columbia area planning. During two successive administrations he was an advisor to the governor's office on the reorganization of Massachusetts state government, serving as the senior staff member responsible for setting up the Cabinet Office of Transportation and Construction.

Mr. Bernard was recently invited to be a member of the faculty of the American Law Institute on the subject of state constitutional constraints on the use of taxation as a land use control.